Constantly Craving

Other Books by Marilyn Meberg

I'd Rather Be Laughing

Choosing the Amusing

The Zippered Heart

The Decision of a Lifetime

Assurance for a Lifetime

Since You Asked

God at Your Wits' End

Free Inside and Out (with Luci Swindoll)

Love Me Never Leave Me

What to Do When the Roof Caves In

Tell Me Everything

Constantly Craving

MARILYN MEBERG

THOMAS NELSON
Since 1798

NASHVILLE   DALLAS   MEXICO CITY   RIO DE JANEIRO

Published in Nashville, Tennessee, by Thomas Nelson. Thomas Nelson is a registered trademark of Thomas Nelson, Inc.

Thomas Nelson, Inc., titles may be purchased in bulk for educational, business, fund-raising, or sales promotional use. For information, please e-mail SpecialMarkets@ThomasNelson.com.

Unless otherwise noted, Scripture quotations are taken from *Holy Bible*, New Living Translation. © 1996, 2004, 2007 by Tyndale House Foundation. Used by permission of Tyndale House Publishers, Inc., Wheaton, Illinois 60189. All rights reserved.

Scripture quotations marked KJV are taken from the KING JAMES VERSION.

Scripture quotations marked MSG are taken from *The Message* by Eugene H. Peterson. © 1993, 1994, 1995, 1996, 2000, 2001, 2002. Used by permission of NavPress Publishing Group. All rights reserved.

Scripture quotations marked NKJV are taken from THE NEW KING JAMES VERSION. © 1982 by Thomas Nelson, Inc. Used by permission. All rights reserved.

Scripture quotations marked NIV are taken from HOLY BIBLE: NEW INTERNATIONAL VERSION®. © 1973, 1978, 1984 by International Bible Society. Used by permission of Zondervan Publishing House. All rights reserved.

Library of Congress Cataloging-in-Publication Data

Meberg, Marilyn.
  Constantly craving / Marilyn Meberg.
    p. cm.
  Includes bibliographical references
  ISBN 978-1-4002-0355-0
  1. Spirituality. 2. Satisfaction—Religious aspects—Christianity. I. Title.
  BV4509.5.M43 2012
  241—dc23   2011040782

Printed in the United States of America

12 13 14 15 16 QGF 6 5 4 3 2 1

I dedicate this book to the memory of my husband, Ken Meberg. For 29 years we laughed, loved, and persevered. For 21 years, I have craved his presence. But the day is coming when all cravings will cease. So get ready, babe. When the time is right, we're going to be laughing together again.

CONTENTS

Contents

Foreword

THERE *IS* A WAY TO FIND THE HAPPINESS YOU CRAVE

ONE OF MY FAVORITE ACTIVITIES AS A PSYCHOLOGIST IS TO READ and study research. It is like a treasure chest to me as I get to see how psychological and psychiatric studies give us a clear picture of what really happens in life. Not that all research is perfect or foolproof, but over time, taken as a whole, it can give us some pretty dependable findings.

Studying research also gives me another exciting result. It sings out to me the truth of the Bible and of the reality of all that God has said to us. Psychological research repeatedly proves the great themes of the Bible and that God's Word truly can be trusted when it tells us about life.

In the last decade, the psychological profession has spent a lot of time, energy, and resources studying the question of what makes people happy. The researchers have looked closely at the differences between happy people and those who aren't, about what will and won't make people happy, and more important, about how someone can change from being an unhappy person to a person who experiences more and more happiness.

The research tells us there are many factors to happiness, including a couple of findings that are relevant to Marilyn's book, *Constantly Craving*. First, the studies tell us that only about 10 percent of our happiness comes from anything circumstantial. But that is not how we usually think, is it? We think, *If I had that job, or that relationship, or lived in that city or that house, or lost twenty-five pounds, or gained a lot of money . . . then I would be happy.* In other words, often when we are unhappy, we think that *more* of something would make it all better.

But research tells us if you get the *more* you are craving, you will return to a "set point" of happiness that has nothing to do with getting more but is determined instead by who you are as a person. It is your basic set point, or "thermostat," of happiness. The big news: getting more is not going to do it for us, no matter how much we crave it.

But all is not hopeless because the second big finding is that there truly is a set of life practices, attitudes, and behaviors that actually will produce the happiness we crave. The lesson is that happiness actually can be found—and increased—in our lives. The cravings can end, and we can become happy and content. However, it is not going to be found on the outside, but from making changes in our hearts, minds, souls, and lives.

That is the answer to our constant craving. It is about walking past the tabloids' seductive promises in the check-out line that lure us into thinking that to be happy we have to look like the latest Hollywood flavor of the week, or have something "they" have. Whether "they" are the cultural icons in magazines, or your neighbor across the street, you must refuse to believe the lie that something "more" on the outside is going to help. Instead we all need to seek the spiritual answers that truly work.

In that arena, Marilyn's book gives us a guide. In *Constantly Craving*, she honestly acknowledges the cravings in life that drive much of our activity, hopes, dreams, disappointments, and even despair. But she doesn't leave us there. She leads us to the reality that a relationship with God and his way of living are the real answers to our deepest longings. And I can tell you that scientific research backs up God's ways as well: they truly work in real life.

My hope for you as you read this book is twofold. First, I hope you will learn that God does have answers for your deepest longings . . . longings for meaning, purpose, forgiveness, relationships, and more. And second, I hope that you will do more than learn. I hope you will put into practice what you learn here. The combination of learning and acting on what we learn embodies the two sides of God's answer to our cravings since day one: faith and action. Faith is to believe what God says about himself and his ways, and action is to put those ways into practice. I believe that if you do both, you will find some answers for some of your deepest longings. And Marilyn's book will be a helpful companion in your journey.

God bless,
Henry Cloud, Ph.D.
Los Angeles, 2011

One

THE ITCH FOR
SOMETHING MORE

EVE, OF GENESIS FAME, WAS (OBVIOUSLY) THE FIRST WOMAN IN recorded history who did not want to be who she was or where she was. She didn't know who or where she would prefer to be, but she knew she wanted more of whatever it was she didn't have.

Her craving for more was elusive and ill defined. She had not experienced *more* but craved it anyway, and that craving drove her to give up what she had in order to get what she didn't even know. The price of Eve's craving for more had catastrophic cosmic consequences; her eviction from perfection left an imprint on all creation. That imprint produced a certain homelessness of the soul that drove Eve, her husband Adam—and all of us who followed—on a quest to return to that place where we hope to find perfection, wholeness, and fulfillment.

Perhaps I need to clarify what I mean by the word *imprint*. An imprint can be compared to a tattoo. Each leaves an impression, one on the flesh, the other on the soul. We all carry the imprint of Eden on our souls. How do we know that? We know it because we all crave wholeness and perfection. It is a universal drive. We humans had perfection once; we want it back. We think we might find it if we could just have more.

This yearning for more leads us to think that wholeness can be found in romantic love, accomplishments, possessions, happiness, fame . . . the list goes on. And so does the craving for more.

The craving shows itself in many ways, ways we may not even recognize as craving. For some it may be reduced to a vague restlessness for which we have no explanation. We may experience it as simply an itch in the soul that we try to accommodate from time to time with a new car, a new house, a new city, new friends, a new lover, a new profession; again, the list goes on. It might be as simple as finding the perfect pizza, one with crust that's not too thick and not too thin.

This book is about recognizing and giving a name to the itch, the quest, the craving for a "more" experience, an experience I think of as finally finding *home*. When we're able to name what drives us, we can study and understand its potential for fulfillment. We can also come to understand its limitations to meet our "more" expectations. My goal in writing this book is to help you learn to live in the balance of a life that does not always meet your expectations—and a life that may sometimes exceed your expectations.

To begin this book's look at our meandering search for

home with its promise of more, I share a lighthearted dinner experience I enjoyed recently with my good friend Luci Swindoll.

The food was good, but the guy playing his guitar and singing what was supposed to be background music was fairly close to terrible. When the musician took a break, he leaned his guitar by the stool and walked away. No one noticed; no one had been listening.

I said to Luci, "I'll pay for your dinner if you'll go over to the guy's stool, pick up his guitar, and sing a number."

She looked at me for only a second. "Dinner?" she asked.

"Dinner," I said.

With the deal made, Luci walked over to the guitar, strummed a few chords, and then began singing "Summertime." The room went totally quiet. The other diners stopped talking, put down their forks, and listened with rapt attention. When Luci finished singing they clapped, cheered, and yelled, "More!"

She couldn't do more; the bet was for one song. (I love it that Luci will do anything for a free meal.)

Why did the people stop talking and eating and start listening? It was not only because Luci has a gorgeous contralto voice. I also think the people were unaware that they needed more quality in the background music. But when they heard it, they thought, *That's it! We needed that!*

Possibly they had been unaware they wanted more of

something; or possibly they felt a sense that something was missing but were unsure what that something was—until they experienced it. Consciously or subconsciously they were looking for a *more* experience. When it happened, they didn't want it to end. Predictably, the diners yelled "More!" when Luci finished singing.

Craving a Supersize More Experience

The desire for a more experience stems from dissatisfaction; we want more of something or other to satisfy the internal itch in the soul that craves something yet to be defined. We all have the itch; we all cast about for ways to satisfy it.

For many of us, the itch for more expresses itself far more dramatically than wanting satisfying background music at dinner. We may crave adrenaline-rush experiences, such as skydiving, bungee jumping, or zip-lining. Or we may crave a more supersize adrenaline experience, something guaranteed to accelerate our heart rate or even threaten our ability to survive.

At this point, I want to confess my own craving for a supersize *more*. As of this writing, I'm seventy-two years old, and I am itching to go zip-lining. I read somewhere that it is currently the fastest-growing outdoor activity for people of all ages craving a more experience.

Let me tell you about this fantastic out-of-the-box-for-even-the-elderly adventure. It involves climbing onto a platform, stepping into a harness, and getting hooked to a cable up to three hundred feet off the ground. Once secured, you go zipping along from one treetop platform to the next at up to sixty-five or seventy miles per hour.

Don't ask me why, but zipping through and over the treetops is enormously appealing to me. In fact, right now I am investigating a particular tour claiming to have the world's longest continuous zip line, spanning five and a half miles, including a 600-foot-long "sky bridge" suspended 170 feet above a gorge. How about *that* for ensuring my heart health by accelerating my pulse rate?

As long as I'm confessing, there's another supersize more experience I love: Brahma bull riding. In this case, you'll be happy to know, I don't crave actually riding the bull myself. I'm happy to be the observer. This craving started when I was six years old and my father took me to my first rodeo in Portland, Oregon. I loved it all, but when the Brahma bulls came into the ring, I stopped breathing. I was mesmerized as a beast weighing more than a thousand pounds leaped, twirled, gyrated, and wildly kicked his back legs into the air in a furious effort to be rid of the tenacious cowboy on his back.

When the cowboy was hurled into the dust, the bull charged the seemingly helpless cowboy with the intent of goring him to death with his horns. But then, as my heart pounded, I saw the rodeo clowns leap into action, hurrying into the bull's line of vision and distracting him from his death-to-the-cowboy intention. The cowboy scrambled away, climbed the arena railing to safety, and it was then I resumed breathing.

The thrill I felt at the age of six, sitting beside my father in the rodeo stands, is still with me. I frequently watch bull riding on TV, but it is far more satisfying to actually be there in person, feeling the crowd's excitement, smelling the rodeo smells, tensing with wide-eyed anticipation as the bull and cowboy go hurtling around the ring.

Understanding the Itch for More

Practically speaking, we know we cannot lead our lives on the adrenaline of supersize more experiences. There's work to be done, children to raise, bills to pay, pipes to fix, teeth to straighten, gardens to weed; the list is endless. If the truth were known, short of the supersize more we occasionally experience, most of us live much like the people in the restaurant, vaguely aware of wanting more of something but not sure what that something is. Sometimes we may happen upon it, but in a short time the gratification is gone and the itch returns.

What is the origin of this craving, this itch in the soul, this relentless questing for more? While living what appears to be a good life, what makes our crabby inner voice some-times whisper, *What is wrong with you? Can't you ever be satisfied?*

Perhaps we also scold ourselves, thinking, *What is wrong with me? Why do I always want more? Will I ever be satisfied? I should feel grateful. Maybe I'm spoiled and self-centered and not even worthy of what I have!* Once that crabby inner voice has a head of steam going, that interior dialogue can continue until we do something toward shushing it—maybe going out and buying something.

In the following chapters we will talk about these mys-terious cravings for more: how they express themselves and how we may better understand them. We'll begin with an examination of the craving for romantic love. Few human experiences knock us off balance more than love. It's a crav-ing that elicits more poetry, music, and drama than any other subject on the planet.

Two

CRAVING MORE ROMANCE

MY MOM NOTICED MY "HAPPY LITTLE FACE" AS SOON AS I SKIPPED in the door. "Was school especially good today, Marilyn?" she asked as I settled in for my favorite afternoon snack.

I knew why I had a happy little face, but I wanted to keep my delicious feeling all to myself, at least until Mom tucked me into bed that night. Then I might tell her my fabulous news: Bobby Turner had told me after kickball that he loved me.

I was ecstatic. I had been eyeballing him ever since he transferred from Camus Elementary to my classroom at Amboy Elementary. He was a little short for a nine-year-old, but he had a certain swagger that made him seem tall. He also had deep brown eyes that melted me. I had prayed all my short life for brown eyes, and here they were, in the cutest boy I'd ever seen. Maybe that was how God was answering my prayer: brown eyes by proxy.

As the days rolled by, Bobby was a steady and loyal keeper of my heart. He always picked me first when we chose sides for kickball, and he complimented me when I scored a run. Each day we walked home from school together and

13

shared half of either his Almond Joy or my Hershey's bar. The seriousness of our relationship was never in doubt.

But then, several months later, I began to find Bobby's swagger annoying. I also decided he truly was too short, with or without his swagger. The fact that I was at least six inches taller than he became an issue.

To my great relief, I didn't have to talk to him about my gradual change of heart. Somehow we started leaving school at different times, and a week later I was sharing my Hershey bar with Jerry Baxter. It was not long before I saw Bobby swaggering home with Norma Delworth.

It didn't cross my mind at the age of nine to ponder why Bobby became increasingly unattractive to me. Neither did I wonder about my relief when Jerry Baxter moved away. Whatever "it" was that caused my feelings to change, both boys no longer had it. At that point in my life, I didn't have the insight to know I was simply experiencing the desire for something more, something else that was surely "out there." I started believing I'd find it later, when I got out of the fourth grade.

The Futile, Furtive Search for Love

The sixteenth-century French writer La Rochefoucauld wrote, "True love is like seeing ghosts: we all talk about it, but few of us have ever seen one." As an optimistic fourth-grader, there is no way I would have believed that crabby assessment of "true love." In fact most of us would think La Rochefoucauld was simply a lonely old Frenchman who had stopped searching too soon and lapsed into a depression.

A case in point is Emma Bovary, the heroine created by another classic French writer, Gustave Flaubert, in his novel *Madame Bovary*. (It sounds as if I'm picking on the French; I'm not. I love croissants.) Emma had high hopes for romance in a perfect and passionate marriage. She describes her idea of how love should be with these words:

> Love must come suddenly, with great outbursts and lightnings—a hurricane of the skies which falls upon life, revolutionizes it, roots up the will like a leaf, and sweeps the whole heart into the abyss.[1]

With those expectations, Emma marries Charles Bovary, a devoted but clumsy and inarticulate country doctor. After a few years of what she perceives as a passionless relationship, she revolts against the boredom and monotony of her life to pursue her romantic dreams.

Until Flaubert's book was written in 1857, the reading public basically agreed with Emma's definition of love as well as her search for it. Those nineteenth-century readers were incensed then when, in Flaubert's novel, Emma never finds romantic love. Instead her sordid and secret affairs are discovered and made public. With her reputation ruined and her scandalous life too hard to bear, Madame Bovary swallows poison and dies.

The reading public was furious, believing Flaubert had let them down. They were used to having their own unmet needs mollified by reading about fictional characters who were rewarded with passion and romance. Why would Flaubert have Emma die under such tragic circumstances when all she wanted was what everyone craves?

Incidentally, after the publication of *Madame Bovary*, other authors began to write novels about life as it is rather than how we wish it were: a perfect existence where romantic cravings are met and cravings for more disappear. Flaubert introduced what became known as literary realism. Poignantly, when Flaubert was interviewed about his tragic heroine, he said, "Emma Bovary is me." His own heart cry was heard in Emma's furtive search for romantic love.

Stage One: High on Romantic Love Drugs

Maybe it would be good to ask whether romantic love is doomed ultimately to disappoint us, fail us, hurt us. Do we inevitably get bored and find someone else to share our candy bar with? Is true love really just a ghost rarely seen?

My answer to those questions is no, romantic love is not doomed to disappoint us, fail us, hurt us, or even bore us. I believe most of us have known a few love ghosts who have not only materialized, they've hung around for the long haul, and we're glad about that. But I do think our eager hearts need to be reminded of some down-to-earth facts concerning love-ghost encounters.

There are two major developmental stages in romantic love. The first stage, the attraction stage, is what knocks us down and drags us around. It's as though we are on a drug high. During the attraction stage the brain releases dopamine and norepinephrine. Those two neurotransmitters produce a rosy outlook on life that also produces an increased pulse rate and increased energy. In addition to those drug rushes, the brain increases its production of endorphins and enkephalins. Those are natural narcotics that make the ghost-spotter grin stupidly and sing in public. And then there's serotonin, yet another serenity-producing neurotransmitter released during the head-over-heels stage. So we can honestly say romantic love *is* initially a drug-induced state of being.

Scientists don't know why the brain releases all those powerful chemicals, and neither do they know why those chemicals diminish with time. It is a biologically documented fact, however, that romantic love pushes all our interior drug buttons.

With that understanding of the chemistry of love, Emma Bovary's definition of love does not seem so extreme.

When she expected "great outbursts and lightnings" and "a hurricane of the skies, which . . . roots up the will like a leaf, and sweeps the whole heart into the abyss," she was describing her love-drug highs. And when that stage of romantic love diminished, no longer producing the high she craved, she assumed she had missed real romance. Therefore the search began again.

Though Emma Bovary is a fictional character, many of us have also fallen victim to her lack of understanding about romantic love. Perhaps we have not known that the first stage of love is a drug high followed by a return to chemical balance. If we assume love is gone when the drug high is gone, we may be missing a good relationship that could develop without the aid of "brain drugs."

Though the brain is at times a dispenser of drugs, it can also become our best friend as it guides us along reasonable ways of being. It can help us understand why we make one choice as opposed to another and why that choice may or may not be wise for us.

The brain serves also as a storehouse of our personal data. Since infancy it has been collecting images of persons who have affected us positively or negatively. Our search for romantic love reaches back to that vast storehouse of images in our brains. That storehouse is where we find the people who have left the deepest brain imprints that have influenced us since infancy. The imprints were probably those of our mothers, fathers, brothers, sisters, or other close relatives. The brain recorded everything about each person's voice, smile, moods, talents, hobbies, the touch of his or her skin, and the look and sound of his or her anger or pleasure.

In addition to those impressions, the brain recorded the various interactions we had with that person—interactions we may not even remember, but they are all recorded nonetheless. Scientists claim we have huge amounts of unrealized information in our brains. Neurosurgeons discovered this fact while performing brain surgery on patients who were under local anesthesia. When certain portions of the patients' brains were stimulated with electrical currents, the patients were immediately able to remember seemingly forgotten events from childhood with amazing detail.

So what does that information about the brain's storehouse of early images and impressions have to do with our constantly craving romantic love? As much as we may dislike this fact, the truth is we are all looking for lovers who most resemble our caretakers; more than likely, our mothers or fathers.

There is a feeling of familiarity when persons we meet either consciously or unconsciously call up old parental images. This familiarity can be positive or negative. In either case the brain fuses the image of the present person with the past caregiver; we then unknowingly transfer our unmet needs for love and nurturance onto the new partner with the unspoken anticipation that finally we have found true love and that we will become the center of our lover's world. We will be heard, received, and regarded in ways that promise a return to the joys of childhood—or even the pain of childhood, but this time the pain will be replaced by consistent and unending love.

To understand what's happening in this stage, let's peek in on another fictional character. I'll call her Bernadette. She experienced the "outbursts, lightnings, and hurricane of the skies" with a lover I'll call Lester. During that phase Bernadette lost sleep from countless hours of conversations with Lester, neither of them able to pull apart because of the depth and richness of their interactions.

Bernadette felt as if she'd finally come home . . . to the place where her every word mattered and her every emotion was important. Lester was more present and compassionate than any human being she'd met before. She could not bear the thought of being separated from him.

Lester, on the other hand, loved the feeling of mattering so deeply to Bernadette, and, since listening was so crucial to her, he gladly became the soothing, kind ear she craved.

Bernadette was the sixth child in a family of ten children. Her well-intentioned parents were overwhelmed with the financial needs of the family and rarely if ever had time to listen to the common "stuff" of her childhood experiences. Bernadette experienced with Lester what she never had with her parents: an available and caring ear. She had years of pent-up feelings, thoughts, and experiences to share, and Lester seemed to delight in hearing about them.

But then Lester became restless. At first he had loved the role of compassionate caregiver. His mother had rarely if ever talked directly to him about anything. She was verbally uncommunicative and emotionally unavailable. In contrast to his mother, Lester felt loved and appreciated by Bernadette. But as he became increasingly aware that Bernadette rarely inquired about *him* and that their long conversations more frequently centered on her life rather than his, he felt almost as shut out, just as he had with his mother. To keep the relationship going, Lester had to deny his feelings. He had to begin playing a role, that of a constantly available person with no needs of his own.

Bernadette picked up on Lester's role-playing and subsequent restlessness and pulled back emotionally, wondering why Lester seemed to be losing interest. Over time, both of them reluctantly concluded that their relationship really was not the love they were craving. They believed that somewhere romantic love must still be out there but with someone else. Sadly, they agreed to go their separate ways.

Stage Two: Accommodating Differences

The unfortunate thing about Lester and Bernadette is that they succeeded with stage one of romantic love but failed with stage two, the crucial stage of becoming acquainted with each other's differences and learning to accommodate them rather than run from them. This is the stage of honest communication where each person risks voicing fears and inadequacies. It is the stage of learning how past family patterns influence our expectations and behaviors for love and relatedness.

It is in this stage that our brain becomes a valued friend, assisting us in making decisions that work for us and not against us. This is a great time to have couple's therapy. Those persons who have relationship therapy are far more likely to build an enduring love life than those who think, *We don't need some nosy-rosy therapist poking into our private lives.*

It is inevitable that both Lester and Bernadette will ultimately follow Emma Bovary on the quest for a new romantic love, believing they can find the one with "outbursts of lightnings" that can "sweep the heart into the abyss."

Acknowledging that probability, we need to learn why we are attracted to some persons and not to others. If we could get that figured out, perhaps our weary hearts could learn to make better choices.

In the next chapter we'll discuss this mystery of

attraction, seeking to understand why we may want more of the short, bald man who makes minimum wage instead of the good-looking guy with money and straight teeth. Surely that doesn't have anything to do with our parents . . . does it?

Three

WHY DO I CRAVE *YOU?*

WE ALL EXPERIENCE A COMPLEX MIX OF PEOPLE WE SEE EVERY day at the grocery store, pharmacy, bank, the mall, work, airport, restaurants, everywhere we go. Sometimes we chat with a few of them, but generally we move quickly through our day without much thought to who attracts us and who does not. Our brain, however, takes in every person we encounter and within nanoseconds discards or selects those few who may be a match either for romance or friendship. This process is based on the contents of our brain's memory-storage system, which says, *That one, not that one.*

For example, we may think, *This person is not safe. That person is overbearing. That person isn't clean. She looks severe. He laughs too loudly. His socks don't match.* The sorting process goes on and on. The strangers don't know they are being run through a personal grid that has been storing images since infancy and producing a save or discard message. Most likely we're unaware of our brain's rapid calculations ourselves. We do become aware of it, however, when someone successfully slides through the grid and gets our attention.

For example, if I am in a social gathering, I'm not drawn to women talking about hair and makeup. But I am drawn to the woman who loves to read. Having unconsciously discarded the makeup woman, I advance toward the book reader, where we may spend time talking about what we are now reading, already have read, what we hope to read soon, and why or how a writer's words charm us. Later in the evening, however, I may find that the makeup woman has a gazillion ways guaranteed to make me look younger and, as if that were not enough, she loves to read!

Our brains sort and discard based on early emotional experiences that create comfort or discomfort within us as we remember them and are unconsciously guided by them.

I was drawn to the book-reading person because her love of books and reading is familiar to me as well as appealing. Many tender reading memories live in my storehouse: my mother reading aloud to my father, who loved the timbre of her voice. Because of those pleasant stored memories, the book reader slid through my grid, and I responded to her.

Another person who slid through my grid was Ken Meberg, one of thousands of Seattle Pacific University students I encountered as a freshman there. I became aware of him as I watched his hilarious performance in the all-school talent contest. He skillfully played a jazzy piano rendition of "When the Saints Go Marching In" while sitting on the bench with the back of his suit cut out to reveal broad, bare shoulders, bright red boxer shorts, and matching red socks.

Bingo! To say I was attracted to this wonderfully zany young man is an understatement. I unconsciously sorted and selected him and then consciously set about devising a plan to meet him. To make a long story short, we were engaged when I was a sophomore and married five days after I graduated.

Choosing One Who Feels Familiar and Safe

How did my parental background influence my response to Ken? To begin with, he was cute. (I think being cute is probably in most people's stored brain files and is not necessarily influenced by parental stuff.) He was an interesting blend of both my parents. As a result, my union with Ken felt familiar and safe.

The matchup of traits looked like this:

- Extremely funny—father
- Sharp businessman—father
- Loved music—both parents
- Valued education—both parents
- Conservative Christian convictions—both parents
- Conservative politics—both parents

- Exceedingly kind and supportive—mother
- Prone to melancholy—mother
- Withheld painful emotions—mother

When I first heard the phrase "we either marry our mother or our father," I interpreted the statement to imply we are insultingly infantile and determined to drag Mama or Daddy around with us for a lifetime. When I ultimately looked at the list of my parents' traits and then those of Ken, however, I had to sit down and shut up. I had married my mother.

True, Ken was a blend of both my parents, but it was my mother who provided me with the most tenderness, compassion, and endless patience. It was also she who was less inclined to talk about her feelings, fears, and other sources of inner distress. Her inclination toward melancholy created in me a deep desire to encourage her and bring her spirits up—in other words, to "fix her."

Like Mother, Ken was wonderfully kind and endlessly patient, and he, too, could dip into a melancholy he didn't want to talk about or even acknowledge. When melancholy set in, I wanted to fix him. I had not been able to fix my mother, so subconsciously I thought it would help me to realize I could at least fix Ken. I loved them both; I fixed neither of them. Their angst was a part of them until they left this life and moved on to heaven, where there is no angst. The fact is, fixing them was not my job. Loving them, with or without fixing, was.

How Knowledge Helps Us Choose

So how does this knowledge that our brain endlessly spits out images from our past help us respond wisely as we consider our future? Can that knowledge be helpful in our choices for romantic love? I suggest it can, and here's why.

After you have navigated your way through the romantic-love drug stage and have settled down to see your lover in a more realistic light, you are entering stage two of romantic love. In this stage you swoon less and think more, and you activate the part of the brain where logic lives.

You can begin this new stage of awareness by asking yourself a few basic questions:

- Who does this lover most remind me of—my mother, father, or another caregiver?
- How do I feel about those similarities and differences?
- If something about him or her makes me feel threatened or unsafe, can I remember what childhood experiences produced those feelings?
- If I feel comfortably "at home" with my lover, do I know why?

- Would my lover be willing to talk openly about these questions?

These considerations are meant to cause you to logically examine the level of personal safety and acceptance you experience in the relationship. If your brain is spitting out images or memories from your past that you recognize as feelings that made you feel unsafe growing up, be aware that you are heading toward a repeat of that experience again.

If that is your situation, realize that you can choose to stop. Love cannot thrive in an atmosphere of threat or rejection. It can thrive with known differences, even differences that may hurt when you realize "I can't fix this," but it can't thrive in an atmosphere that says, "You won't survive this."

Thriving means flourishing. Marrying my mother, along with a good smattering of my father here and there, implied that my emotional environment should be free from threat. To the degree it is possible in an imperfect world, my romantic love had every logical reason to flourish.

Using Logic to Guide Your Choices

Now let's talk about you. Let's say a person who has a temper slides through your grid. It takes a while for you to realize his temper can at times be violently expressed by yelling, pounding walls, breaking glass, and slamming doors. This trait is troubling to you, but it's also familiar. Your father's temper was frightening to you. There were many days throughout your childhood when you, your two sisters, and your mother were terrified. You say he only hit your mother once, but the image of her bloody face still lives in your memory.

Logic asks, *Why would you choose a relationship with a person who has a bad temper? Don't you remember the feelings of threat you experienced as you were growing up? Do you remember the looks of fear, insecurity, and helplessness you saw on your mother's face? Do you realize you are on the verge of marrying your father? Why would you choose to repeat your past?*

As we discussed earlier, there are two major reasons why you choose to relive your past: First, that past, though hurtful and often threatening, is at least familiar. You lived through it and survived it. And second, this time around, you will "fix" your father (lover). Unlike your mother, who was weak and gave up too easily (in your opinion), you are strong. You almost owe it to your mother's memory to get it right; you will do what your mother was unable to do. By rewriting the pages of your hurtful past, you picture yourself enjoying a hurt-free future.

Logic asks, *How in the world are you going to rewrite your history by changing or fixing your lover?* And your response is, *I love him enough to do it; I trust in the power of my love.*

Maybe at this point it would be beneficial for us to define the terms *love* and *romantic love*. My *Dictionary of Psychology* defines *love* as "an intense feeling of fondness or attraction, deeper and stronger than liking, especially when associated with a romantic or sexual attraction to someone."

It defines *romantic love* as "the need to be with the loved person, willingness to make sacrifices for the loved person and a desire to be intimately involved with the loved person to the exclusion of others."[1]

The phrase "willingness to make sacrifices for the loved person" could imply that your logic of fixing your lover's inclination to violence is commendable. Actually, your response is neither logical nor commendable. It is instead an unhealthy tolerance of destructive behavior. We must recognize that familiarity attracts us, but logic must direct us. If we are not safe, we will not flourish.

There is another kind of love that is more likely to provide safety as well as fulfillment, and that is *agape love*. *Agape* is the Greek word for "brotherly love." This kind of love is one of mutuality; I give to you in love as you give to me in love. This kind of love is not one-sided. The apostle Paul spoke of the mutuality of agape love as he instructed husbands and wives how to show that kind of love to each other. In Ephesians 5:25 he told husbands to "love your wives, just as Christ loved the church. He gave up his life for her."

Ephesians 5:28–30 provides further instructions on how a man is to love a woman: "Husbands ought to love their wives as they love their own bodies. For a man who loves his wife actually shows love for himself. No one hates his own body but feeds and cares for it, just as Christ cares for the church. And we are members of his body."

We women are instructed to return the love of our husbands with the same selflessness they show to us. This love, romantic love, is one of sweet expressions of caring for the needs of each other.

Psalm 97:10 dogmatically states, "You who love the LORD, hate evil!" Love cannot flourish in an evil environment; nor can it flourish in a violent environment. We are to love ourselves as Christ loves us. Christ loves us tenderly, consistently, and protectively. We must do the same for ourselves. Logic tells us to avoid abusive behavior; Scripture tells us to hate it.

Questioning Logic

Let's return to the question we heard logic asking earlier: *How in the world are you going to rewrite your history by changing or fixing your lover?* And let's consider your expected response: *I love him enough to do it. I trust in the power of my love.* Now tell me, is that response illogical, naïve, or unrealistic? Is it contrary to Scripture, which tells you to "hate evil"?

My answer is that yes, we are told to hate evil, but that does not mean we don't try to find solutions for it. As Christ followers, we are called to be light in a dark world; evil is the source of that darkness.

That being said, I would not recommend the choice of an abusively angry man as a mate. Love, even one committed to bringing about light and change, cannot flourish under threat. Your mother tried. My opinion is not that she was too weak but that his darkness was too strong.

It is also important to say that this prone-to-violence lover is certainly not a lost cause. There are therapies that examine the root causes of behavior that, if he commits to them, can bring about behavior changes. My suggestion would be that he agrees to those therapies before you commit to marrying him. And his first motivation must be a genuine desire to tackle his anger issues for his own sake. It cannot be simply to win you in marriage.

Four

CRAVING MORE FROM MARRIAGE

BEFORE WE DELVE FURTHER IN TRYING TO UNDERSTAND OUR relentless craving for more, let's review what's been said so far. We've said there is a dimension in all of us that craves excitement. We may not crave bungee jumping, skydiving, or zip-lining, but we want something—sometimes an unidentified something—to break the monotony of our sameness. We want something more than we are experiencing.

One of the most exciting *more* experiences is in the area of romance. When the drug high of romantic love whirls us around, we feel alive, invigorated, and, yes, intoxicated. When ultimately the high no longer exists, we settle into the next phase of romantic love, a stage that is more practical and down to earth. In phase two we learn whether or not we want to continue the relationship. Many people in this stage assume they have "fallen out of love," so they go in search of the next possible love-drug high—the chemical imbalance that usually accompanies the first phase of love attraction.

If we decide to stay with the love that at first whirls us around, we come to understand that there are personal selection grids through which potential love candidates enter, causing us to feel attracted to them. At first we may not necessarily be aware of this brain-selection system, which is based entirely upon our early emotional experiences since infancy. When we come to understand how the grid works, we can more clearly understand how we come to marry our mothers, fathers, or other primary caretakers. This understanding need not be embarrassing or demeaning; it is simply how the system works.

When we come to understand ourselves this way, we can begin to work on healing what didn't work for us in the past and move on to living in a more balanced interior world.

Our Powerful Craving for the Cradle

To understand how our constantly craving more impacts the marriage relationship, we first need to recognize the fact that we are created for human contact. The longing for touch and connection is built into us at birth.

I will never forget the rush of feeling I had when my infant son, Jeff, curled his little fingers around mine and didn't let go. When I held him, stroked him, and cuddled him close to my body, he relaxed and grew quiet. Next to food, water, and oxygen, the human organism craves contact.

The kind of contact we crave becomes more complex and specific as our bodies mature. Soon the infant fingers curling around Mama's fingers are not enough. As the budding person grows he or she wants more of what was received in the cradle: constant touch and adoration. It may seem embarrassing to acknowledge as adults, but we all long to return to the security and nurturance of the cradle. We don't outgrow that longing, although we may get good at denying it to ourselves and disguising it from others. And, of course, those who were on starvation rations (not getting enough contact) feel a greater and possibly more obvious need. Those persons may even be willing to risk everything—their marriages, their families, their homes—in their effort to find it.

Many persons unaware of the deeper root of this desire for contact, this cradle-craving, may simply decide they married the wrong man or woman. At first the relationship looked promising and even exciting, but when stage two of romantic love settled in, the cradle-craving spouse decided the connection just wasn't there after all. In spite of the heartbreak and disruption that comes with divorce, this person may cling to the hope that he or she *can* find the right mate and finally settle into wedded bliss.

Thus the uninformed search for romantic love continues as the cradle-craver's quest pushes him or her into another relationship . . . and then another. Eventually the hope of finding a "real" connection dies, and the cradle-craver may come to the reluctant conclusion: "I'm not cut out for marriage. I'd be smart to remain single."

So what's the big deal about the cradle? Why does it

exert such power over us, and why do we long to return to it? Who in their right mind can imagine an adult body scrunching into a cradle space? Long, hairy legs and arms dangling to the floor with fingers tensely clutching the TV remote is not a pretty picture. (I realize this is a male image; forgive me.)

What did the cradle offer that we continue to crave? Human contact. The crying baby needs to be held, fed, cuddled, and stroked. Contact restored the baby's emotional equilibrium, and with that equilibrium came a sense of trust that all is right with the world; it is a safe place after all.

No matter how old we get, we desperately crave a safe place where relief from threat, pain, loneliness, insecurity, and hunger is assured. What better place than the cradle to reexperience the meeting of our primary needs?

And where does an adult find the familiar warmth and security of the cradle? Sometimes it's in the arms of a new lover. Of course, the adult cradle-craver has the added need for sexual satisfaction. That kind of contact adds a new and powerful component that makes the cradle an even more appealing space.

Okay, we may reluctantly agree that to be a cradle-dweller has an appeal. We understand we long to be assured of getting our needs met with nothing more than a convincing cry. The idea we can then be rocked back to a place of gentle assurance, that we are indeed utterly adorable, and life was without meaning until we arrived is almost too good to be true. Incidentally, it is not only men who are cradle-cravers; women are as well. And why not? A "cushy" life has great appeal.

Risking Everything for More Love

Recognizing our deep longings to reexperience infancy satisfaction may partially explain why some people risk everything for more love, but there is also another explanation. It is disappointment with the marriage partner.

Whether it takes a few months or a few years, sooner or later the realization hits: *You're not the person I thought I married.*

At that point, logic asks, *Well, who did you think I was?*

The wounded answer: *I thought you would be the one who always would make me feel attractive, confident, secure, and lovable. I thought you would always yearn to be with me and no one else. I thought you would think what I said and did were always wonderful and that you couldn't imagine anyone doing or saying anything more pleasing than what I say and do.*

Logic asks, *Why do you assume I'm no longer that person?*

The wounded answer: *Because you have become distant. You spend more time with other people and have endless activities that don't even include me. Now we go to bed to sleep and not to make love. I'm lonely.*

As we discussed earlier, people unconsciously marry with the anticipation that the new spouse will do what had not been fully accomplished in childhood:

- *Mother loved me, but when she went back to work she became preoccupied and too busy. She didn't have time or energy for all my basketball games, dance recitals, field trips, or swim lessons.*
- *Dad loved me, but he rarely complimented me or made me feel I excelled at anything. He usually told me to try harder and do better. He helped me buy my first car, but he didn't have time to teach me to drive it. I longed to hear him say at least once in my life "good job."*

The newly married couple anticipates that their spouse will now meet their previously unmet needs:

- *Mother was too busy for me, but you won't be.*
- *Dad did not compliment me, but you will.*

Why the expectation? The courtship seemed to promise it. So why aren't these needs being met as we expected them to be?

They go unmet because our agendas have changed. Each spouse now has the same expectation: *I need you now for me and my needs, not for you and your needs.*

The resulting disappointment causes each partner to pull back, disappointed and disillusioned, and bury the hurt with outside activities.

Divorce or affairs are not the answer to the heart's cry for more love. Neither is pulling away and becoming emotionally disengaged, the situation that occurs when couples stay together but the spouses have separate lives running along parallel tracks. There may be less friction and fewer hurtful accusations with that arrangement, but there is little intimacy. That lack of intimacy makes the spouses vulnerable to falling for someone new.

The Wisdom to Make Smart Choices

So what's the answer? I believe we need a better understanding of why we feel, think, and behave as we do. We need a better understanding of ourselves before we can have a better understanding of our marriages. In other words, I need to examine *me* before I give up on *thee*.

To begin with, I was born a precious baby. So were you. Each of us was—and is—a miracle of creation. But from the very beginning of life, we each wanted more. Mama and Daddy could have given up food, water, and sleep for two straight years to tend to us constantly, and it would not have been enough.

And as we went through each developmental stage,

we wanted more emotional nurturance than we received. Sometimes we truly deserved more than we got, but even if we had gotten what we deserved, it never would have been enough.

Ultimately, we each developed into a person old enough to marry. And what are we looking for in a spouse? Someone who can give us *more*.

How do we make that happen? We find someone like our primary caretaker, who will fall in love with us, marry us, and then make up for all the times Mom was too busy and Dad was too unavailable.

Incidentally, all these maneuverings are unconsciously motivated by the hungry little person inside us.

So once we understand that we are and will continue to be insatiably needy human beings, what next? We use that wisdom to make smart decisions. Knowledge produces clarity of mind, which inspires logic. We can choose to live differently than our more primitive nature dictates. We do not need to foist our neediness upon our spouse. We can seriously set about giving agape love to him or her instead of pouty criticism. We can make new and better choices.

But as we make those new and better choices, a little voice may rise up from the floor of our soul and quietly say: *Whadya expect from me? I'm a cradle-craver. I'm not even sure I know how to make better choices. The fact is, this chapter has made me feel pretty cranky. Reading it has filled me with more shame than encouragement. I am who I am—and have no idea what to do about it.*

Well said, little voice. I understand, and I want to remind you that all human beings have the same basic needs; those needs are not shameful. Understanding them, tracing their origins, and choosing not to allow them to victimize us is a great beginning. It is also the beginning of knowing the one who says, "I am who I am and have no idea what to do about it."

Five

LONGING FOR
CONTENTMENT

I GOT MILD WHIPLASH THAT DAY ON THE PLAYGROUND WHEN MY best friend Barbara looked me square in the eye and said, "I wish I was you!"

We were both five years old; I did not know her comment was grammatically incorrect (my mother would have said Barbara was using "subjective mode contrary to text").

I said, "Huh?"

"I mean it," she said. "Your life is better. I want to live your life."

She went on to say she was sick of her three-year-old twin brothers hogging all of her mama's time. Because I was an only child, she knew I got a whole lot more attention than she did. She also said my mama was really sweet and probably never yelled. Barbara said everything at her house was noisy while everything at my house was quiet.

"And," she added, "your daddy makes me laugh. I love to laugh, but nobody laughs at my house."

I lapsed into a deep think. It was true my house was very quiet, but in my opinion that wasn't always a good thing. I had always wanted siblings to play with even if they were noisy. Sometimes I was lonely.

I liked Barbara's mother well enough, but her father was hardly ever home, so I didn't have a real sense of him except that he always wore bib overalls. I thought they were a poor fashion choice, but it didn't mean I could never like him.

I whiplashed again when Barbara suggested we exchange lives; she would become Marilyn, and I would become Barbara. She would move into my house, and I would move into hers. Of course, we had to run this by our parents, and amazingly enough, they agreed.

We packed our meager belongings into little suitcases and exchanged houses. This was a simple action since we lived across the street from each other.

The minute I arrived and became Barbara, I loved it. The twins were adorable and tons of fun and obviously thought I was a far better sister than Barbara. Everything was great . . . until bedtime.

I had not known Barbara and the twins shared a bedroom. The twins fussed, cried, demanded more and longer drinks of water, and climbed out of bed, refusing to get back in until Barbara's mother yelled, "Enough!" and threw the boys in bed, stomped out, and slammed the door.

I was stunned. Being Barbara at bedtime was not the peace-producing experience it was at my house, where my mother always read me a Bible story before bed. Then she would pray out loud and thank Jesus for always being with me.

That night I crawled out of Barbara's bed and walked quietly into the kitchen where Mrs. Pederson was doing dishes. It took her a while to notice me, but when she did she said, "What do you want, Mar—I mean Barbara?"

I asked her if maybe she could read me a story or something. Her response was, "Honey, I don't have time to read you anything; just tell yourself a story."

The next morning Barbara and I decided to move back into our own houses. She wasn't used to a Bible story and prayer before bed. She didn't like the story and thought it was spooky to close your eyes and talk to someone you couldn't see. Barbara was afraid that Jesus, whoever he was, might be hiding in the closet and would pop out when my mother left the room.

Barbara had been sure she'd experience more contentment at my house; instead, she had less. At five years old, we were both too young to know contentment is an inside job and that changing our circumstances, or rejecting who we are in the hope of living someone else's life, doesn't work.

Soul Swap

That basic truth was satirically illustrated in the movie *Cold Souls*. The offbeat comedy appealed to me because, well, I love offbeat comedies. In the movie, actor Paul Giamatti plays an actor named Paul Giamatti who is desperately searching more contentment.

As the movie begins, he is totally *without* contentment and suffering a midlife and midcareer crisis of anxiety and neurosis that manifests itself in his inability to play the title role in Chekov's play *Uncle Vanya*.

After a near breakdown at rehearsal, Paul's director advises him to take a break and go home. Despairingly, Paul sinks into the familiarity of his La-Z-Boy recliner and then notices a magazine article, which he reads and comes to think may hold a solution for his present state. The article described a high-tech company that extracts, deep-freezes, and stores people's souls in a minivault. (I told you it was offbeat!)

To investigate the procedure, Paul travels to Roosevelt Island, where an empathic doctor affirms his quest; he tells Paul a twisted soul is like a tumor—better to remove it. So Paul has his soul removed and replaces it with the soul of a bored Russian dancer selected from the mini-vault catalog.

Ultimately, Paul wants his old soul back, and the movie revolves around his difficulty in finding it. He learns it was sold to a Russian company that had discovered there was money to be made in the soul-trafficking business.

Cold Souls is a delicious example of social satire, an

outlandishly zany way to get our attention and then make a serious point by knocking us off balance. Satire causes us to cock our heads and think about something we may have skipped over all our lives as just another ordinary *yeah, yeah, yeah* idea. Effective satire helps us get the point and then remember it by creating a lingering intensity.

In the movie Paul tries a solution born of desperation; we feel sorry for him because we can identify with his desperation, which brings us to recognize one of the major deterrents to contentment: we don't want to live our own lives. We want to live someone else's life because we think it has more contentment.

Paul believes the solution to his desperation is to get to the root of his problem by finding or buying a new soul. But that solution does not help him. Like Barbara and me, Paul wants to return to what's familiar even though it was not satisfying in the past.

Reformulating Mind and Soul

Actually, Paul was closer to a solution than he may have realized. And so are many of us when we're desperately seeking contentment. The solution *is* a new soul, but of course we don't find it at a high-tech company on Roosevelt Island.

First let's consider what the soul is. In the New Testament the Greek word for soul is *psueche*, which is translated as "psyche." *Unger's Bible Dictionary* defines *soul* as "the seat of our feelings, desires, affections and aversions," and the *Dictionary of Psychology* defines *psyche* as "the human mind or soul."

Based on those definitions, I'd like to suggest that the soul (the psyche) is our interior being (our mind and soul) from which our emotions and behaviors have their origins. If we were to find a new soul, we would need to replace those old emotions and behaviors with new ones that work for us and not against us.

Perhaps the most dramatic acquisition of a new soul is spoken about in the life of another Paul, the apostle Paul in the New Testament. He was a highly educated, oratorically gifted Jewish-Roman citizen and leader, and he was incensed by the rapid growth of a movement that promoted Jesus as the Son of God who had risen from the dead three days after his crucifixion. Even though more than five hundred witnesses claimed to have seen Jesus before he ascended to heaven with the promise to his disciples that he would return, Paul was determined to save the world from this fanaticism. To Paul, the honor of God and the Jewish faith demanded one thing: the extermination of all Christians. His soul (his mind and emotions) was unshakably committed to this quest.

The spread of Christians to foreign cities fueled Paul's

fire and extended the scope of his activities. But one day, as he approached Damascus, armed with the authority from the Jewish high priest to arrest and persecute Christians, the transforming crisis in Paul's life occurred. The event can be described only as a divine intervention. We read about it in Acts 9:3–6:

> As he was approaching Damascus on this mission, a light from heaven suddenly shone down around him. He fell to the ground and heard a voice saying to him, "Saul! Saul! Why are you persecuting me?"
>
> "Who are you, lord?" Saul asked.
>
> And the voice replied, "I am Jesus, the one you are persecuting! Now get up and go into the city, and you will be told what you must do."

Paul, after three days of blindness and fasting, completely rethought his opposition to Jesus. In fact, he spent the next several years reformulating his mind and emotions about who Jesus was, is, and continues to be in the life of the believer. With a new soul, Paul became one of the world's most influentially powerful voices in the growth of the Christian faith and in establishing the Christian church. With the same mental convictions and emotional drive that had fueled Paul's opposition to Jesus, he gave his life to being a witness for Jesus.

The Steps to Contentment

Paul was not only a witness for Christ, but he was also—and continues to be—a witness and an example of contentment. His sense of contentment is nearly unbelievable in view of where he spent much of his life. Because of his zeal in communicating the good news of Jesus, Paul spent years in prison. Those who had an earlier loyalty and allegiance to Paul and his zeal to persecute Christians turned on him, arrested him, and ultimately executed him in Rome. And yet, while sitting in jail prior to his execution, Paul wrote these words:

> I have learned in whatever state I am, to be *content*: I know how to be abased, and I know how to abound. Everywhere and in all things I have learned both to be full and to be hungry, both to abound and to suffer need. I can do all things through Christ who strengthens me. (Philippians 4:11–13 NKJV, emphasis mine)

Paul's words provide a simple but profound definition of contentment. Shockingly, it has nothing to do with our circumstances. Most of us assume if we could just change our circumstances we would be content. If I were Paul, I might have said, "Just get me out of jail, and I'll be content."

But he said contentment didn't depend on whether or

not he was in jail, whether or not he was hungry or had just eaten a platter of pasta. He knew contentment is an inside job. His trust and faith in Christ got him through it all.

Contentment like Paul's is compelling. We wonder how Paul got it—and can we get it too? If Paul got a new soul, is it possible for us to get a new soul as well? Let's examine the steps Paul took and see what we can learn for ourselves.

- First, he believed: Scripture says, "There is salvation in no one else! God has given no other name under heaven by which we must be saved" (Acts 4:12). Jesus made himself known to Paul, and Paul chose to believe that only Jesus is the source of salvation. Paul had to reject all former systems of thought and belief.

- Second, he received: "You can pray for anything, and if you have faith, you will receive it" (Matthew 21:22). Paul had to act on what he believed. His belief could not be passive; to *receive* is an action. Prayer is acting on the decision to believe.

- Third, he confessed: "If we claim we have no sin, we are only fooling ourselves and not living in the truth. But if we confess our sins to him, he is faithful and just to forgive us our sins and to cleanse us from all wickedness. If we claim we have not sinned, we are calling God a liar and showing that his word has no place in our hearts" (1 John 1:8–10).

- According to the Jewish standard by which Paul had been raised and professionally trained, it would initially have been a huge issue for Paul to believe he was a sinner. He had kept the commandments, observed the Jewish holidays, and worked conscientiously to serve God. When Paul realized he had murdered countless Christians, however, he referred to himself as a sinner saved by grace. Confession and then forgiveness "cleansed him from all wickedness."

- Fourth, he became committed to the Christian faith. Paul said Christians "must be committed to the mystery of the faith now revealed and must live with a clear conscience" (1 Timothy 3:9).

Paul embraced the new Christian faith wholeheartedly. Living with a clear conscience was a familiar admonition.

Forgiven, Cleansed, and Made New

These were the steps Paul took to gain a new understanding of Jesus and receive a new and transformed soul. His old soul was forgiven, cleansed, and made new. Paul described this newness: "Anyone who belongs to Christ has become a new person. The old life is gone; a new life has begun!" (2 Corinthians 5:17).

When Paul experienced his transformed, cleansed, and forgiven soul, he came into an understanding and experiencing of contentment. Because of the forgiveness with cleansing from sin, Paul could walk without the shame and guilt of his murderous past.

Since the mind is a part of the soul, Paul had access to the mind of Christ, who said, "Let this mind be in you, which was also in Christ Jesus" (Philippians 2:5 KJV). Christ's mind in Paul's mind reminds him that Christ promises to never leave him. Christ's mind assures Paul's mind his love will always hold him up, providing courage for each experience that hurts him, threatens him, or discourages him.

That's how Paul's transformed new soul enabled him to sit in jail, even knowing he would ultimately experience execution, and still say, "I have learned in whatever state I am, to be content."

I am encouraged by the words "I have learned." They tell me we are not born content, and achieving contentment does not happen quickly. It's something we learn. As our relationship with Christ develops over time and through experiences, we learn to trust God more and ourselves less. Through the indwelling Christ I learn that contentment is an inside job.

I can also learn that my old soul is in need of transformation, and there is a way to receive a new soul. Jesus makes that possible; Paul's Damascus road experience teaches me how. That *Cold Souls* doctor was more profound than he knew when he said, "A twisted soul is like a tumor—better to remove it."

Six

HUNGRY FOR
HAPPINESS

LISTEN IN ON THE FOLLOWING CONVERSATION: "MARILYN, WE just found a perfect personal ad for you. It reads, 'Professional man seeks the company of a professional woman. His most attractive quality: contentedness.'"

Wordlessly I stare at my friends as they follow up with another personal ad they also think worthy of my response. "Successful and handsome man looking for a mature relationship: frequently described as a 'happy guy.'"

I continue to stare at my friends. "Say something, Marilyn!" they demand.

So I begin with my testimony that they have heard before: "I am not looking for the company of a happy or contented man. I'm not looking for anyone. I don't have the time or inclination to develop a romantic relationship at this stage in my life. I don't want to take on someone else's grandchildren or his peculiar habits ingrained by years of repetition, and I don't want to learn to cook like his first wife did. I've hardly learned how to cook, period." (I point to my kitchen counter, where a decorative pillow reads, "I only have a kitchen because it came with the house.")

Just between you and me (that sounds so ungrammatical, I know), I have to admit there *was* something rather provocative about those two ads, but it had nothing to do with whether I was inclined to respond. The points of interest for me are the potential questions the ads raise. One guy is content, the other happy.

Is it possible to be content but not happy? Is it possible to be happy but not content? What is the difference between the two statuses, and should that difference matter to the rest of us and not just to the person who answers the ads? I think the answers can provide valuable clarity for our *more-*craving souls.

Can a Happy Person Be Content?

Contentment is a state of being that is characterized by not wanting more than we have. A contented person is basically satisfied with life's circumstances. On a spiritual level, we, like the apostle Paul, can be content with life knowing we have a transformed soul and God has sovereignly ordained our circumstances. Because we trust God, we can be content to leave it all to him.

But on a human level, being content with our circumstances and having no desire to change them can at times be incomprehensible—simply beyond our understanding. For example, I wonder how a pig can be content to snort around in garbage and wallow in the mud? That is incomprehensible to me. Why? Because I'm not a pig. Pigs, however, were meant to find contentment in that environment.

Then how can a human being be content to live in a filthy environment with rodents scurrying around everywhere? That's equally incomprehensible to me. Why? Because it's not my idea of contentedness.

Yet, as incomprehensible as that is to me, the apostle Paul lived in a jail cell with rodents scurrying around everywhere and said he was content. His statement reminds us again that contentedness is an inside job; it comes as the pig lives out the destiny for which it was created, and it comes to you and me as we share Paul's trust in God's timing and sovereignty.

Now let's talk about the word *happy*. We know it is an adjective that describes a feeling. And we know that feelings are never constant; they can change dramatically or unexpectedly. So is it possible to be content and also happy? Of course it is, but happy moments come along as additions to the state of contentedness. While he was imprisoned, Paul experienced moments of happiness when he received a supportive and loving letter from the outside. Being happy was a bonus to the contentedness he already felt.

So, can a happy person be content? Actually, no—at least not without some groundwork.

Let me explain: a person experiencing the feeling of

being happy without the grounding of contentment is only going to continue living a craving-for-more existence. That's why I'd never go for the guy who is only happy. If he has no foundation of contentment, he will blow around the universe in search of more happy feelings. He's got the order wrong. He must first find contentment; then he can enjoy the happy moments that come and go throughout a lifetime.

Differing Definitions of *Happy*

It would seem that answering the question "What is happiness?" should be simple. After all, everyone wants it, experiences it, and recognizes it. But the fact is, there are thousands of books on happiness, and most start their discussion with the question "What is it?" Almost all find happiness difficult to define. Why? Because everyone experiences happiness differently.

We know happiness is a feeling based on an experience; that experience may make one person happy but not another. We also know the feeling of being happy is a relatively brief elevation of mood that for one may be slurping ice cream while for another it's organizing a closet.

Recently I read about another example of differing happy feelings in the story of a Pennsylvania man who is refusing to take down a twenty-four-foot-tall illuminated cross he built in his front yard. The cross builder says its size demonstrates his religious conviction, but officials say the cross violates local ordinances and shines into neighbors' windows. The cross builder says the size of the cross represents the size of his faith; just looking at it makes him happy. The neighbors, however, don't share his happy feeling.

Happy Connectedness

As I was watching a TV account of conjoined female twins, I had to reeducate myself to remember that conjoined twins are babies whose embryos did not separate completely during fetal development. The result is the birth of two babies who remain physically connected to each other when they leave the womb.

The twins in the TV report are fused at the shoulders; they have two heads with separate, fully functioning brains but only one trunk, two arms, and two legs. Because they have separate brains, they have differing thought processes as well as differing personalities. Both twins are effervescent and charming; one is a little more outspoken than the other, but their mother says they usually live in harmony with their differences.

At the time of the televised report, they were just turning sixteen, going to a public high school, talking and giggling on the phone. They like boys, play on a softball team, and are taking driver's education with the anticipation of getting a driver's license.

In spite of all those normal teenage activities, the twins are obviously physically challenged, and there is no clear-cut medical precedent to follow as they develop into adulthood. As a result, their future well-being is medically uncertain. Nevertheless, both twins are certain about one thing: they do not ever want to be surgically separated. When asked why, each said she loves knowing the other is there.

To know they will always sleep together, laugh together, eat together, and cry together is a source of enormous comfort to them. I was jolted as they both looked into the camera and one said, "Doesn't *everyone* long to be connected to someone she loves? Well, we are naturally connected, and we make each other happy."

What was startling to me as a viewer of the show was that I could not imagine their connection produced happiness. My thought was, *You only think you're happy because you've never known anything else. We almost always choose the familiar to the unknown.* And yet, what right do I have to decide what constitutes their happiness?

The Drive to Feel Happy

My reaction to the conjoined twin's statement reveals one of the problems with searching for a definition of *happiness*:

we don't always agree on its source. That lack of agreement leaves us with a definition that usually begins, "Well, it's that certain feeling when . . ."

Though we may not experience happiness as a result of the same experiences, the human race is still highly driven to feel happy. All philosophies since Plato discuss the primary purpose and intention of life as the search for happiness.

Seventeenth-century philosopher Blaise Pascal said all persons seek happiness. It is the motive of every action of every person. Nineteenth-century researcher Sigmund Freud also stated that the purpose and intention of life is to be happy—and ideally to become increasingly more and more happy.

Thomas Jefferson not only felt that striving for happiness was important; he believed the "pursuit of happiness" was our national birthright. As such, it was written into the American Declaration of Independence in 1776. He believed the main business of the state was to provide for the happiness of those governed.

The craving for more happiness ranks right up there with the drive for more romance. Both cravings can be relentless drivers; we will go to almost any length to satisfy those urges. If we agree with Jefferson, the drive to achieve more happiness is more than human craving; it's a civil right. (Perhaps that makes it more commendable than the craving for more romance.)

What Makes Us Happy

So far, in an effort to answer the question "What is happiness?" we can only say, "It's not clear." We know it's a feeling that produces a pleasurable elevation in mood, we know it does not last indefinitely, and we know that what makes one person happy does not make another happy. We also know that for centuries great minds have written about how the pursuit of happiness is one of humanity's greatest *more* cravings. That's a lot of hot air and black ink devoted to a subject no one seems able to nail down!

To add even more ink to the illusive and ill-defined subject of happiness, I'm going to make a few suggestions of my own, based on seventy-two years of living, searching for, and experiencing happiness-producing moments.

To begin with, I love to laugh. Laughing makes me happy. A good joke makes me happy and can elevate my mood again and again because I can keep telling it to myself. When I was a child, there were three jokes I told myself at night after my mother read to me, prayed with me, tucked me into bed, and then turned out the light. These three jokes never failed me. I told them to myself in the same order, always leaving the same last joke for my heartiest laugh.

We lived in a small house, so my parents would hear me telling myself the jokes, chuckling at first and then finishing with a great guffaw at the end. Dad would say, "She just told the fish joke." Quiet would then descend upon my bedroom, and soon I was asleep.

Not only do jokes make me laugh, *I* make me laugh. I do and say some really dumb things. Of course I have a choice in how to respond to those dumb things: I can be disgusted and chastise myself, or I can laugh and say, "Bless your heart, honey."

Recently I locked myself out of the house. I encouraged myself with the fact that I had hidden a house key in a sandwich baggy and slipped it into a crevice of the brick wall on my patio. Smiling at my brilliant preparation for just such a lockout, I scanned the wall for the crevice and the tip of my baggy peeking out.

Nothing. After scanning several more times, I gave up and called Luci on my cell phone. (Fortunately, it was in my pocket.) "Do you have any idea why I can't find my bagged house key in the crevice of the patio wall?" I asked her.

Without skipping a beat she said, "You decided not to leave it there because the baggy poked out."

"Really? Do you know what I did with it?"

"Yeah, it's in your garage on the third shelf where you hide things."

"Wow, I don't remember having a shelf devoted to hidden things."

"Well, you do."

I found the key behind the Weed B Gone.

"Wonder why I would hide the weed killer . . ." I mused to myself before adding, "Bless your heart, honey."

Enlarging Our Potential for Happiness

In two previous books I've authored, *I'd Rather Be Laughing* and *Choosing the Amusing*, I suggest the establishing of a laugh-lifestyle. Laughter and the ability for choosing the amusing rather than self-defeat is a deliberately chosen attitude of the mind. In fact, there is a direct correlation from our attitudes to our ability to experience happiness. One of the most crucial attitudes we can develop is one of gratitude. A grateful attitude in itself produces an elevation of mood. When I see my circumstances through the lens of a grateful mind-set instead of the "I'm not getting what I want" mind-set, I feel better; I even have the potential to be happy in spite of circumstances.

As I write this, we North Texans are just crawling out of an especially severe winter. There were four days when most of us dared not leave our homes because of ice and snow. On the fifth day following our confinement, I inched toward the grocery store for relief from peanut butter sandwiches and shared a moment of happiness with a woman who looked at me over a pile of fresh tomatoes and with a teary voice said, "These tomatoes make me so happy!"

I experienced many other moments of gratitude

during that snow-and-ice storm: my pipes did not freeze, my electricity did not go out, my furnace continued to function, my phone worked, and even that beast (the computer) in my home office remained vigilantly alive and well. I was grateful.

My encouragement that you develop an attitude of gratitude may be so familiar that you simply respond, "Yeah, yeah. I've heard that before." But I suggest we all (myself included) hear it again. Keeping a "gratitude list" may sound corny, but it redirects our mind and lifts our mood. Write up a list of everything for which you are grateful: the big stuff and the little stuff.

Here are a few sources of gratitude on my list today: the side door no longer sticks, I located more of my favorite hard-to-find vanilla loose-leaf tea, birds are singing again, the new water filter makes the water taste better, my lamp throws light perfectly on my book. And at the top of this list is the greatest source of my gratitude: Jesus loves me.

Hopefully our lists go on and on. If they do, we enlarge our happiness potential.

Expect Less, Get More

Another attitude I suggest we look at is our level of expectation from the events in our lives. I've often heard it said, "Expect more and you get more," but I think if we expect *less*, we get more. I know this sounds counterproductive to positive thinking, but let me explain why I think this way.

Let's assume you had a high expectation for your family vacation. But on the second day out, two of your children come down with stomach flu, which quickly spreads to everyone else in the family. In addition to that, you have a flat tire, ruin the tire driving on it, and your spare is flat.

No one is happy.

How could lowered expectations for this trip have helped your happiness potential? You know sickness is always a possibility, so while hoping against it you prepare for it anyway, packing medicine for the trip. When the flu erupts, you and your family are grateful for your provision. Your car's tires are showing signs of wear, so you make sure your spare is aired up and ready to go before you leave, and you also carry a can of flat-fixer. Plus, you bring along the Old Maid cards to play while you're waiting for the flat to be fixed, increasing the happiness of your children because you inevitably picked the Old Maid card.

Expecting less does not mean we prepare less, we try less, or we are less determined to live out our potential. It means less can become more, and when that happens, it produces happiness!

Since our craving for more happiness is a well-documented universal preoccupation, it may comfort us to know there are ways happiness can become a more frequent and less elusive experience. It is often a choice based on wise and knowledgeable reasoning.

In his excellent book *The Law of Happiness*, Dr. Henry Cloud says only 10 percent of our happiness is due to personal circumstances; 50 percent comes from our internal makeup, and the rest is determined by us.

That being the case, I recognize my deepest happiness can only be found in the God who created us to know him, love him, and trust him in all things. As Pascal wrote, "Happiness is neither outside or inside us. It is in God, both outside and inside us."

Seven

NEEDING MORE
FROM FRIENDSHIP

ALL HUMAN BEINGS CRAVE THE EMOTIONAL INTIMACY THAT comes with friendship. We are not created to live in isolation from one another but to experience connection. That inborn need to connect drives each of us to seek out persons who seem inherently wired to understand us, support us, and even delight in us. That sense of kinship causes us to feel recognized and validated, no longer isolated.

Since the craving for friendship connection is a simple truth, many of us were surprised and then delighted by the news accounts of an unusual and tender friendship that developed between a hundred-year-old tortoise and a baby hippopotamus. This unlikely relationship sparked enthusiastic interest around the world. The friends' photographs have appeared in countless newspapers and magazine articles, television programs, and even a documentary film. I was utterly charmed by the image of that old tortoise being lovingly nuzzled by the baby hippo. I wanted to know more. Here's the backstory as described in the book *Owen and Mzee.*[1]

On the morning of December 26, 2004, an earthquake in the Indian Ocean produced a giant tsunami that sent waters rushing high onto the beaches of the small town of Malindi on the east coast of Africa. After the tsunami, the villagers saw a baby hippopotamus, without his mother, stranded on a sandy coral reef among the sea grass. Tired and frightened, he was unable to reach the shore on his own. Knowing he would become sick if he stayed in the salty seawater too long, hundreds of villagers began working together to bring him to shore. They used ropes, boats, fishing nets, and even cars to try to haul him out of the water.

This was no small effort since the baby weighed somewhere around six hundred pounds, was slippery, and furiously opposed being netted or roped. Finally a rescuer named Owen tried a stronger shark net, and Baby was successfully towed to land and hoisted into the back of a pickup truck.

No one was sure about the next step for the extremely cranky hippo in the pickup truck. After some research and a few phone calls, it was decided he would be taken to Haller Park, an animal sanctuary near the city of Mambasa. The manager of the park offered to "create a comfortable home" for Baby since he had never learned survival skills and would not be safe out in the world. Baby was named "Owen" in honor of his primary rescuer and was driven about fifty miles to his new home.

During Owen's ride the sanctuary workers quickly set

about preparing a perfect home for him in a large park enclosure complete with a pond and mud wallow surrounded by tall trees and brush. A few other animals lived in this "home," one of whom was a giant Aldabra tortoise named Mzee (a name that in Swahili means "wise old man").

Mzee's contentment was drastically eliminated when his circumstances produced an unwelcome change, a baby hippo who came to live with him.

Owen arrived weak and exhausted, but as soon as the ropes that held him were untied, he rushed from the truck directly to Mzee in what appeared to be an effort to be safe. In response, Mzee hissed indignantly and crawled away.

Owen followed. Mzee hissed again and kept crawling. It didn't take much energy for Owen to continue following Mzee. Finally, as it began to get dark, Mzee stopped hissing and crawling. Owen then snuggled up with the no-longer-content tortoise, and they spent their first night together.

Over the next week Mzee continued to crawl away from Owen, but he did stop hissing. Then, interestingly enough, a change occurred. When Owen would walk away from Mzee, Mzee would follow.

Mzee gradually went from feeling hostile to hospitable. The evidence of that was Mzee's encouraging Owen to eat. The caretakers were worried Owen would not survive since he wouldn't eat any of the leaves left out for him. But then Mzee came alongside Owen and started eating the leaves, which prompted Owen to imitate the tortoise's eating behavior.

As the weeks went on, Owen and Mzee spent more and more time together. Ultimately they were inseparable. According to the park caretakers, their bond was not only expressed in swimming, eating, drinking, and sleeping together but also in frequently rubbing noses. When Owen nuzzled Mzee's neck, the old tortoise stretched his neck forward in a gesture indicating a *more* craving. They followed each other to all corners of their enclosure.

A touching reality of this story is that both animals could easily injure each other, but their behaviors continue to be gentle and caring; they trust each other.

Lessons Learned from Owen and Mzee

This recent and well-documented event is reminiscent of those ancient stories called fables: short, moralistic tales that usually include some kind of lesson learned from the experiences of personified animals. A fable is a kinder, gentler way of communicating a truth. With that in mind, I'd like to point out some of the moralistic lessons about friendship we can learn from the experiences of Owen and Mzee. I'll list a few of these lessons, and you can see whether any lessons speak to you:

- Be willing to provide comfort, security, and shelter to one who is weak and exhausted.
- Be willing to pursue a potential friend even if he or she is not responsive.
- Be willing to alter your contented circumstances and embrace a new person with whom you think you have nothing in common.
- Be willing to teach by example.
- Be free to express appropriate physical expressions of caring.
- Be aware that we're never too old for a young friend.

Since I was raised in a pastor's home, I frequently witnessed the offer of comfort, security, and shelter for those who were weak and exhausted. That's what a Christ follower is supposed to do. How much, then, should we do for an exhausted friend in need of comfort, security, and shelter?

I have a wonderfully kind and generous neighbor who is experiencing some major health challenges. Among the many friends dropping by with food and other offers of help is an especially vigilant friend who is incidentally a fantastic cook. I happen to know this because my neighbor is not eating much and says I'd be doing her a favor if I helped her consume some of the food. Of course I feel motivated to be of service.

I have since learned a bit more about my neighbor's friend, perhaps learning one of the reasons she is so vigilantly loyal. The friend's husband was a doctor, as was my neighbor's husband. They socialized together for several years with no knowledge that the friend's husband was stealing drugs from the hospital; they just knew he was becoming increasingly irrational and physically abusive.

One morning around two o'clock, my neighbor and her husband rushed to the friend's house and rescued her from the husband, who was ranting, "I'm going to kill you!" The friends hid her on their boat for three weeks, protecting her from her husband.

Amazingly, this horror story had a happy ending as the doctor sought professional help for his addiction and was ultimately reunited with his wife.

Boundaries and Trust

My point in sharing the story of my neighbor and her friend is that she provided security and shelter in her friend's time of great need. Rarely are we called to provide the kind of assistance my neighbor's friend needed. But a good question to ask ourselves might be, *How much are we willing to alter our lives to help a friend?* And perhaps we should also ask ourselves (of course, using common sense in our response), *Do I have limits? What are they? Should I commit to more . . . less? What is the right balance for me . . . for my family?*

Jesus is an encouraging example of one who recognized that the humanity he chose to experience came with built-in limitations. In his human form he could not meet the needs of every worthy person who was weak, exhausted, and in need. He did not lack compassion, but he lacked stamina.

We read in Mark 3:9 how Jesus placed a boundary between himself and the crowds by climbing in a boat, pushing away from the shore, and teaching the people from the boat. Sometimes we, too, need to get in a boat and push away from the shore. That may at times be common sense for us.

On the other hand, let's consider how willing we are to pursue a potential friend even if he or she puts distance between us and is not responsive to our offer to help—or even hisses at us, as Mzee responded to Owen. Granted, this kind of pursuing is difficult to do. Generally, if someone is not responsive to our offers of friendship, or responds negatively, we assume he or she doesn't like us. That hurts our feelings and threatens our sense of worth. There is no doubt the personal-grid system I talked about in chapter 3 is in play here. You may simply not be a person who conjures up familiar and happy memories from the past in the other person. Not getting through his or her grid may have nothing to do with who you are and the richness you could bring to a friendship.

When a person is unresponsive to me, I first consider the personal grid that basically assures me it's not about me but about that host of "thems" in the other person's early background. Then I consider the reasons a person might be hesitant or even afraid of emotional intimacy. Being friends requires an emotional commitment, and many persons would rather live in isolation than risk the potential hurts of friendship. They may have been betrayed, abandoned, or made to feel inadequate by friends in the past. Or they may live by the old adage, "You can hurt me once, but you can't hurt me twice." When we hurt, we lose trust. It seems to make sense then that if we want to avoid hurt, we won't trust anyone or commit to friendship.

If we feel driven to pursue an obviously unresponsive person, we need to recognize the possibility that the person has trust issues from past hurts. We then need to prove ourselves trustworthy, a trait that can be evidenced by the observable way we treat others. Kindness in our behavior accompanied by words of kindness when we talk about others is a step toward trust building.

Perhaps an obvious word of wisdom about pursuing a potential friend who is not responsive was stated by my friend Pat Wenger's ten-year-old grandson Carson, who said, "Mom, I don't want any more friends. I have four, and that's all I can handle!"

Making Friends by Embracing Change

To be willing to alter your contented circumstances and embrace a new person with whom you think you have nothing in common is admittedly a challenge. Most of us are resistant to change. As my fourteen-year-old grandson Alec said, "I've got my life arranged and I don't want to change it." These words were literally hurled at my daughter Beth as she, Alec, and his brother Ian discussed the possibility of having a foreign exchange student live with them for six months.

Beth loves change. She picks up stray animals or people and is challenged by new ways of living life. The idea of offering her home to a seventeen-year-old boy named Marcin from Poland, who wanted to graduate from an American high school, appealed to her on all levels of her expansive heart. Sixteen-year-old Ian thought it was a cool idea because he knew the boy from the previous exchange home he had been in for six months. In Ian's words, "He's a good athlete, has a great sense of humor, and is not a dork."

These qualifications convinced Ian the plan would work, but Alec felt it was doomed to fail. Why? Because

Alec didn't know Marcin and did not want to know him. "I don't speak Polish or understand Polish. How can I ask him to even pass the salt?" he said.

Alec is a very orderly, disciplined young man who has all his ducks in a row. Do not even think of rearranging those ducks! The upside of the proposed plan, however, was that Alec could move downstairs to the guestroom. That meant he no longer had to share a bedroom with Ian. Giving up his bed to Marcin and moving downstairs sealed the deal for Alec.

Hearing about Alec's change in attitude toward Marcin has been fascinating to me. Alec is in the gifted programs in school and now is excited to learn about Poland and its rich history and language. Not only that, but Marcin is teaching Alec some new strategies in chess.

In a few weeks Marcin will be returning to Poland. Recently Alec told Beth he can't stand to even think about it.

Marcin taught Alec more than new strategies in chess. He taught him that one of life's greatest gifts is to experience friendship in unexpected places and at unwanted times.

Teaching Friendship by Mentoring

Perhaps the most obvious way to teach friendship by example is to become a mentoring friend. Admittedly, the word *mentoring* can feel inhibiting because it is defined as "a wise and trusted counselor or teacher," and given that definition, many of us may not feel qualified.

All Mzee had to do to teach by example was eat leaves; Owen got the picture. But when I consent to a mentoring friendship, I need to mirror far more than the art of leaf consumption.

One of the basics of mentoring is to start where the person is on issues of development. I cannot expect the friend to know more than she has been taught. Owen did not have a mother; he did not know the simple basics of eating. Mzee started at the place of Owen's greatest need.

I had a mentoring friendship with a woman who had many security issues. She found it hard to believe I genuinely cared about her. If I invited her to lunch, she struggled to believe I really wanted to be with her. She always prepared herself for a cancellation call from me at the last minute. I had to become an example of one who was dependable, one who always showed up and expressed my pleasure in being with her.

It was helpful for me to understand my friend's grid, which screened her contacts through a childhood that had rarely known stability. People left when they should have stayed, forgot when they should have remembered, and showed up only if it was convenient. All those experiences communicated one message to her: you do not matter. To get through the ride, I needed to continually mirror to her how much she mattered to me.

Expressing Physical Caring

Feeling free to express appropriate physical expressions of caring is a thorny issue in our society now. For example, a teacher must be cautious about hugging, patting, or touching students. Touching behaviors can be reported as provocative, leading to public censure and a possible lawsuit. On the other hand, there are instances when the touching behavior has been truly inappropriate and needed to be reported. The result of these widely reported negative incidents is an understandable restraint from expressing physical caring.

I found it interesting to learn that the tradition of shaking hands had its origin in an intention to ensure personal safety. If you shook the hand extended to you and did not feel a gun, you could relax, knowing you were safe from being shot. If you were too worried about your safety to shake hands, you were described as being gun-shy.

Today we all still need to be gun-shy at times. On the other hand, many opportunities for appropriate human connection are lost when our anxieties keep us away from each other. No longer trusting each other's intentions causes a society to become suspicious and withdrawn. The purpose of friendship is connection, an antidote for isolation.

Owen and Mzee nuzzled. I suggest we hug. A warm hug is a soft reminder that I am cared for, highly thought of, and worthy of your esteem. I think it's worth the risk.

Friends of All Ages

Since all living, breathing creatures are created for connection, we, as humans, can benefit from connecting with persons of all ages. The fact is, we're never too old for a young friend . . . or too young for an older friend.

One of my favorite young friends is Lisa Whelchel. Among other movie and TV roles, she is perhaps best known as Blair from the *Facts of Life* television series many years ago. Because we work together as authors and speakers with Women of Faith, I know her not only as a media personality but also as a treasured friend.

Lisa is the age of my daughter Beth, but we soon learned the age difference between us was irrelevant. She is one of those kindred spirits who cause my soul to leap in recognition. We have spent hours simply mulling over the deep issues of life: what makes us laugh, cry, yearn, experience satisfaction; what causes one soul to leap and another to stay in place; what was God thinking when . . . The list goes on, as does the mutuality of our kinship.

The friendship between old Mzee and young Owen was established very differently than that of old Marilyn and young Lisa. Mzee hissed and crawled away; Owen followed anyway. I did not hiss or crawl away; Lisa did not need to follow. Instead, we met in a common and pleasant enclosure, minus the mud wallow, where we simply came to know each other. Age was not an issue; it was merely a backdrop for soul commonality. So, speaking from experience, I can say we're never too old for a young friend. Our bodies age, but our souls remain young. My legs may no longer leap, but my soul can.

When friendships are richly rewarding, does the itch in the soul still make itself known with its familiar craving for more? To answer that question, ask yourself this question: *Do I have any friends from whom I don't want just a bit* more?

Eight

I DON'T HAVE TIME!

THE "WITHERED HAUNCHES OF THE ELDERLY" IS A DESCRIPTIVE phrase that looms up at me when I pass a full-length mirror. Equally distressing is the phrase "relentless ravages of time." Those last words spring to mind when I check my chin for pasta sauce that leads then to a quick glance at my teeth, lips, and neck. None of this mirror activity is comforting.

This morning an irritatingly cheerful woman leaned into a TV camera and said to me, "You can take ten years off your face. There's no reason not to look as good as you feel." I looked at her perfectly redesigned face and wondered if she'd ever suffered from irritable bowel syndrome.

The human body is a walking, talking clock. We take a look and can read fairly accurately how many ticktocks have transpired. Maybe with some effective plastic surgery we can throw off the clock reader by a decade, but with the continual ticking, some of us "Big Bens" may choose to return for more repair.

Unlike their parents and grandparents, who generally crave more time in their lives, our little Bulova-faced children desperately want the ticktock speed to increase. They want to be old enough to go to school, get a driver's license, buy a car, leave home, get married, have a baby, and qualify for a mortgage. Then, with enough ticking, they, too, become Big Bens with faces that reflect the many ticktocks they've lived through. And maybe they, too, then start sensing the familiar itch for *more*.

To those persons deeply committed to looking "forever young," time is not a friend. Its persistent presence is not only reflected on their faces but in their bodies as well, causing them to wonder, *Why do I have hip pain? Why are stairs a challenge one day and not the next? I can't believe the flesh waving from the backs of my arms. What is there to wave about, and why the exuberance?*

Internal Clocks, Tightly Wound

Time not only dabbles with our physicality but also with our souls. As we age we may reflect on various times when we wish we'd said something different or lived life differently. For me, those wishes most often center on memories of the way I mothered my children, forever hurrying and forever requiring it of them.

I remember with a stab of guilt when my son Jeff, then five years old, told me he didn't like my watch. I was surprised because it was a beautiful watch, a Christmas present from Ken. "Honey, why do you not like my watch?" I asked him.

"'Cause every time you look at it you tell me to hurry up," he answered.

I realized the truth of his statement. I was then, and am still, a slave to my watch. Actually, I'm a slave to time. It is a sad realization that I continue to be driven from the same old internal imperative, *Hurry up! You have places to go and things to do.* Or, *If you don't hurry up, you'll be late.* That one really gets me because I like to be on time; when I'm late, or think I may be late, I become tense.

It is interesting to me that Jeff now owns several companies, all the product of his creative entrepreneurial mind. He is never late and never misses an appointment. And he does not wear a watch.

I've asked him how he knows what time it is without a watch. He smiles and says, "I have an internal clock, Mom." I think I scarred him for life.

I, too, have an internal clock; it is wound tightly and ticks loudly. My fidelity to time is an advantage to me in that I'm dependable and don't keep people waiting. But it is a disadvantage when I become enslaved to it.

An overly conscientious awareness of time can thwart meaningful connections and blind us to opportunities to help people. When we're enslaved to time, a phone call from a friend can be looked upon as an unwelcome interruption because it throws off the timing of my carefully planned day. Mercy! It might mean my to-do list stares accusingly at me at the end of the day with the charge, *You did not finish!*

Taking Time to Do the Right Thing

I have wondered at times what I would do if I were faced with the challenges of the good Samaritan, who stopped to help a badly injured stranger lying by the side of the road.

Would I first think, *If I stop, I'm going to be late for my appointment?* The point of this parable told by Jesus was primarily to illustrate the kindness of a Samaritan who saved the life of a badly injured Jewish man. Because of the centuries-old prejudice Jews felt for Samaritans, it was a notable example of kindness.

For some of us, the parable illustrates an additional lesson: the need to simply take time to do the right thing, the kind thing. It encourages us to rethink the degree to which we may be enslaved to time.

Recognizing that possible stumbling point for people who mean to do the right thing but buckle under their self-imposed time constraints, a study was done with some seminary students. Two psychologists met with the seminarians and asked each one to prepare a sermon on the parable of the good Samaritan. Each seminarian then was told to walk to a building only a few blocks away and give his sermon to a waiting audience.

On the way to the building, each of the seminarians saw a bloody, battered, and moaning person lying in an alley, the intended assumption being that the person had been the victim of some kind of street crime. The seminarians did not know this was a staged scene. The psychologists were not only testing the degree of their humanitarian instincts but also the degree to which those instincts were influenced by time constraints.

The researchers sent each seminarian over to the building with different instructions. Persons in the first group were told to hurry because they were starting out later than planned. Persons in the second group were told they need not hurry because they were a few minutes ahead of schedule.

The results of this study revealed that those who thought they had more time stopped to help the "victim." The other group literally stepped over the victim in their haste to get to the building on time and deliver their sermon on the good Samaritan.

Staging a Time-Prison Jailbreak

Second Peter 2:19 convicts me with these words: "You are a slave to whatever controls you." Since I own up to the unattractive fact that I am all too often enslaved by time, what can I do to get out of my watch-shaped jail cell? I am currently working on a jailbreak this very minute. In case you're interested, I'll share my strategy.

Proverbs 23:7 says, "As he thinks in his heart, so is he" (NKJV). It's telling me that when I want to change my behavior, I first have to change my mind. What I *think* is usually expressed by what I *do*. So I settle down and listen to what I'm thinking. This is a crucial part of the jailbreak strategy.

As I've already confessed, I'm generally thinking, *Hurry up! You don't have time.* Here's an example of that thinking and how I hope to break free of its imprisonment, at least in one instance. As I write, my daughter Beth's wedding is coming up. And a little more than three weeks after the wedding, the manuscript of this book is due to the publisher. At this point, I am less than halfway through the writing process. No doubt about it, I'm running behind.

My plan is to fly to Beth's house in Ohio three days before the wedding and return back to Texas a week later. During those seven days I will attend the wedding as well as celebrate my grandson Ian's sixteenth birthday. These are two fantastic events. I adore my daughter and am thrilled that, after being a single parent for ten years, she is marrying a man who also adores her. He is kind, intelligent, generous, and patient. His steady dependability provides security not only for Beth but for my mind as well. Bottom line: I trust him with my daughter and two grandsons.

I'm also excited to participate in Ian's sixteenth

birthday, a hugely significant time in his life when he can legally drive me to the grocery store down the street (or into the elm tree on the corner). He has a darling girlfriend (who thinks I'm cool), and he is surrounded by fun-loving but responsible guy friends. I love the energy of his "crowd" and want to experience it.

So what's the problem, Marilyn? Why do you need a jailbreak strategy?

I need it because my typical time-enslavement thinking says, *You do not have seven spare days to spend with Beth and her family. You need to arrive the day before the wedding and leave the next day. You need those extra four days to write.*

But in response, my jailbreak strategy thinks, *Are you crazy, Marilyn? You need to spend a few days with Beth before the wedding. You may be called upon for sage prewedding advice. And you need to luxuriate in that time in Beth's soon-to-be old house and cap off sweet memories in it before she moves into Dave's house. And not only that, Marilyn, it is unthinkable to miss your grandson's sixteenth birthday, and you would miss it if you went home early. Beth has witnessed your not-enough-time enslavement all her life. What a gift you now have the opportunity to give to her and her firstborn: your unhurried time.*

So okay, then: I'm convinced. I am spending a full week in Ohio, and while I'm there, I'm not even going to think about writing. This is a moment in time when I choose to be fully present. The watch-shaped jail cell will

stay in Texas. (I have to have a place to leave my unfin-
ished manuscript.)

I truly can change my thinking about time, and it is
possible to change my behavior as a result. Those are soul
efforts over which I have some control. Though my arms'
waving flesh does not yield to think-change, there's hope
for my soul.

The words of T. S. Eliot speak a haunting confession:
"I have measured out my life with coffee spoons." My jailbreak strategy says I can choose to change that.

Using Our Time Wisely

We have a higher calling on our lives than mere dribbles
from coffee spoons, or even the completion of multitudinous
tasks we assign ourselves. Psalm 90 asks the God of the universe to "teach us to make the most of our time." In that
psalm is God's unfathomable measurement of time: "A thousand years are as a passing day, as brief as a few night hours"
(v. 4). God is not bound by time; we are.

Since we do not have a thousand years, we ask what
then we should do with the allotted time we do have.
Knowing how to wisely use our time on earth requires us
to determine meaning and purpose for our very existence:
*Why am I here? What does it all mean? What is my personal calling?
How much does God figure into all this?*

The Golden Rule

Those are huge issues to contemplate and will be the subject of a subsequent chapter. No less huge is a suggestion about how to "do" our dailiness. Jesus reduced it all to what is known as the golden rule, usually recited as "Do unto others as you would have them do unto you." It's based on Luke 6:31.

There is no doubt that if everyone on the planet followed this rule, we could live out our time in harmony and peace. But some people didn't get the memo, and as a result, harmony and peace are rare commodities for most cultures.

Too often the world's thinking seems to be, *I want your oil-rich land, so I'll fight for it. I want your technological formulas, so I'll steal them. I want your power, so I'll manipulate to get it. I want your money, so I'll cheat you out of it. I want your wife, so I'll seduce her.* The list is endless, and the golden rule is nowhere to be seen.

In contrast, our daily lives offer plenty of opportunities for living out the rule simply and quietly: water the neighbors' plants during their vacation, walk the dog until a friend's leg heals, take hot meals to shut-ins, donate food to a food bank and clothes for the homeless. Again, the list is endless.

Sometimes, however, living out the rule is a bit more dramatic than walking the dog. Last week I drove into my garage about 10:40 p.m.; ten minutes later my doorbell rang. I froze. No one rings the doorbell at that time of night. The drapes were not pulled; I could be easily seen if the doorbell ringer walked around the house and looked through the windows.

I quickly walked into a corner of the kitchen and scrunched down next to the microwave oven where I could not be seen as easily. The doorbell rang again. *Someone saw me come into the garage and into the house. That someone is ringing my doorbell.*

My purse was within reach; I pulled out my cell phone and texted my ever-helpful next-door neighbor, Bonnie Prusak.

"Are you up?"

"Yes. Why do you ask?"

"Has anyone rung your doorbell within the last five minutes?"

"No. What's going on?"

"Someone just rang my doorbell twice."

"I'll turn my outside lights on and look out."

Soon she texted back, "I don't see anyone outside. I'm going to call the nonemergency police and have them drive through the neighborhood. Stay by your microwave!"

Ten minutes later I heard nothing, saw nothing, and had a leg cramp from scrunching. Then I walked to the front window and saw Bonnie talking with my neighbors John and Fran Wachs in my driveway. Bonnie had called them to see if they had received any "doorbell threats."

They had not but felt the whole thing worthy of investigation. John walked around my house but saw no one hiding in the bushes or running from the backyard.

As we stood there talking I remembered a pizza delivery car had been behind me as I drove down my street. We decided he did not have the correct address for his delivery, knew that I was up, and thought maybe I'd ordered a pizza. That train of thought had led him to ring my doorbell.

I don't know for sure if that scenario explained the doorbell threat, but I do know this: three caring and protective neighbors came to my rescue. They extended the golden rule to me, and I will be forever grateful.

Several Women of Faith speakers and staff members live in the same suburban Dallas neighborhood, which we call the Women of Faith Frisco campus. We all share a creatively competent landscaper named Kipp Milliron, who faithfully superintends and nurtures our grass, flowers, trees, shrubs, and anything else that grows in the ground. Kipp told me a poignantly tragic golden-rule story involving a good friend and his wife, whom Kipp had known for thirty years. The couple lost their son in a drunk-driving accident three days before Christmas. As the boy was driving home from college for the holidays, he was hit head-on and died at the scene of the accident.

A few days later, as Kipp was driving away from the boy's graveside service, he noticed a small note card fluttering along the ground. He stopped the car and chased after it. It was a picture of the mother and her deceased son taken in happier days. In lovely script written at the bottom of the card were the words, "Merry Christmas, dear son . . . I will love you forever."

The card was originally intended to accompany a bow on a Christmas package. Instead, it was placed on a funeral wreath at the graveside. It blew off the wreath, and Kipp snatched it up. For a while he wondered how to return the card. Should he just go to their home and say, "I found this blowing in the street"? Or should he mail it to them so they could grieve its return privately? It was such a significant card Kipp decided to take it to our favorite framer (whose shop is also on our Frisco campus) and see what she thought might be done to commemorate it. Sherry suggested lasering the card onto a ten-inch-by-ten-inch piece of black granite.

Everyone loved the idea; the finished product was stunning. Of course, the parents were emotionally overwhelmed but they were also deeply touched by Kipp's creative thoughtfulness. It was such a sweet "do unto others" gesture.

There is a definite personal payback when we "do unto others." It feels good to extend kindness beyond ourselves. I think we have that inborn reward system because we are designed to do good things for others. I think God embedded that instinct within each one of his creation because yielding to it is a good use of our time.

The Most Supreme Use of Our Time

The most important way we can use our time wisely is related to another instinct shared by humanity, the yearning to believe in a being or an object that we perceive to be greater than ourselves. Since the beginning of time, all cultures have had some kind of faith system. Saint Augustine's God was the God of the Bible, the God who created heaven and earth and all the people who have lived or continue to live on the earth. This God shares a yearning with his people; he yearns to have a relationship with each of them. Saint Augustine famously wrote about God's intent, "You God have created us for yourself, and our hearts are restless until they rest in you."

I came to a personal understanding of God's love for me and his desire for a relationship with me when I was five years old. I had not been aware of a yearning or a restlessness. Life was uncomplicated by lofty questions such as how to use my time wisely or whether God was invested in anything about my time.

Since Dad was a pastor, I heard about God a lot—we prayed before meals and bed—but I didn't really think about him. I didn't think about him, that is, until Leroy

Walker, my turtle, died. I was devastated and for the first time experienced the never-to-live-again reality of death. Leroy's death raised questions like, "What happens when I die?" "Where do I go?" "Where is Leroy?"

My mother explained to me that I need not fear death because there is a place called heaven where I will go and where God lives. When I die he will take me to that perfect place, and I will live there forever. She also said she wasn't sure about Leroy Walker, but God seemed to value animals because he made so many—and who could imagine a perfect place without animals?

With Mother beside me, I prayed a simple prayer accepting Jesus, the Son of God, who came to this earth to die for the sins of the world. I didn't fully understand it all, but I knew I had made a deal with God: I would love him, and he would love me forever. With that, we started the relationship God yearns to have with all members of his creation. It was real to me then; it is real to me now.

It's easy to start a relationship but not so easy to maintain it. A relationship takes time. It requires preferential treatment. I must choose the relationship over other possible time-stealers and distractions. I must commit to feeding that relationship by communicating my soul: talking about my pain, wants, wishes, and desires. I need to stay current in relationship and not drift off and lose focus.

Since time is crucial for the maintenance of a relationship,

I have to determine in my never-enough-time mind-set to set apart time for my God relationship. It must be time when the phone, doorbell, morning paper, *Good Morning America*, and any other good thing does not take me away from time with my Creator. On those days when outside distractions succeed in keeping me from my God time, I suffer a bit. I don't lose my relationship, but I lose the richness that would have come from the quiet time I missed. Psalm 27:8 states:

> My heart has heard you say,
> "Come and talk with me."
> And my heart responds,
> "Lord, I am coming."

How then should we use our time on this earth? If you desire to ease the look of passing time with a face-lift, tummy tuck, eye lift, or whatever else can provide that adjustment, go for it. There is no scripture I'm aware of that says, "Thou shalt look thy age."

However, there *are* many scriptures that encourage us to love and serve one another whether or not we have time for it.

And in addition to loving and serving each other is the admonition, "Thou shalt love the Lord thy God with all thy heart, and with all thy soul, and with all thy mind" (Matthew 22:37 KJV). That is the supreme use of our time.

Nine

YEARNING FOR MORE MEANING IN LIFE

MY STUDENTS IN WORLD LITERATURE CAME INTO OUR EIGHT o'clock class looking disgruntled. An 8:00 a.m. class is reason enough to look and feel disgruntled, but their faces registered emotions deeper than the early morning hour. One of the young men who often served as class spokesperson started by saying, "I really don't have a clue what this play is about. It frustrated me to read it; it also made me mad."

Other students chimed in: "It's a stupid play." "What is it supposed to be saying?" "Why is it famous?" "It totally makes no sense." "Who is Godot?" "Why doesn't he show up?"

They were responding to Samuel Beckett's play *Waiting for Godot*, and their feelings were understandable; there is no meaningful dialogue action or resolve in the play. The reason why Beckett had been awarded the 1969 Nobel Prize for literature was mystifying to them.

The play opens with two poorly dressed, possibly homeless men named Vladimir and Estragon waiting beside a desolate road. They are waiting for the mysterious Godot. The waiting is agonizing.

At the end of the day, Vladimir and Estragon resign

themselves to the fact Godot will not come that day. They think maybe he will come the next. The play depicts the meaninglessness of their time spent in waiting. They meet new people as they all walk down the road—toward what or whom is not clear.

To pass the time, Vladimir and Estragon tell each other jokes, do pointless exercises, get bored, and then quit. The final curtain drops as Vladimir and Estragon sit by the side of the road. They think maybe today is the day Godot may come.

My class ultimately got into a spirited discussion on who Godot might represent. Was he God? Were the men waiting for Godot to give meaning and purpose to their obviously impoverished lives? How did they hear about Godot, and why were they sure he was worth waiting for? One insightful student suggested Beckett meant to raise the question of meaninglessness in the lives of many human beings and that maybe a lot of people are waiting beside roads of their own choosing. My spokesperson student said grudgingly, "I guess making me feel frustrated with his play was a good way to tell me that's how a lot of people feel about living."

The Despair of Meaninglessness

Beckett's depiction of life as meaningless, with the poignant longings of those who do not give up waiting for

116

it, is noteworthy. The topic of meaninglessness has been written about and pondered for centuries. Shakespeare's Macbeth said,

> *Life's but a walking shadow, a poor player*
> *That struts and frets his hour upon the stage*
> *And then is heard no more: it is a tale*
> *Told by an idiot, full of sound and fury,*
> *Signifying nothing.*
>
> —*MACBETH*, ACT 5, SCENE 5

David wrote that "we are merely moving shadows, and all our busy rushing ends in nothing. We heap up wealth, not knowing who will spend it" (Psalm 39:6). Then, as the psalmist makes these observations on what is purely human, with no consideration of the divine, he quickly directs his heart from the *meaninglessness* of human life to the *hope* for human life, concluding with, "And so, Lord, where do I put my hope? My only hope is in you" (v. 7).

Beckett's play could inspire us to consider where, or in whom, we place our hope. Vladimir and Estragon placed theirs in the mythical Godot, with whom they had no relationship. To them, and to many others, it seems safer to hope in the elusive or the unattainable so there is no need for commitment. These people prefer to continue in a state of questing for meaning because it keeps them occupied with what seems, to them at least, a respectable spiritual journey.

C. S. Lewis described his own spiritual journey as one where, prior to *believing* in God, he merely *theorized* about God. He thought an impersonal God would allow personal freedom and a relief from commitment. That was appealing to Lewis at the time. He also pondered whether there might be a God of beauty, truth, and goodness inside our heads that also was appealing and required no personal commitment. Or perhaps there was some kind of life force that could be accessed and used for personal benefit whenever one chose. That, too, was attractive.

But, he further speculated, what if God makes himself known to us? What if he knows us, and it is possible to know him? Then all our dabbling in religion and questing to find meaning in life could be frighteningly reduced to "God found me before I found him."

That realization caused Lewis to yield to the wooing, seeking heart of God.

Solomon, the writer of Ecclesiastes, said there was no longer the drive to find meaning in God. He knew God and had been raised to love and revere God; but Solomon gradually rejected the God of his youth and increasingly descended into a life of godless hedonism.

Solomon was the second son of King David and Bathsheba. When David died, Solomon became the third and last king of a united Israel. He built the kingdom to its greatest geographical extension and material prosperity. Through a series of marriage alliances, one of which was with the daughter of the king of Egypt, Solomon became increasingly wealthy. Women were a serious weakness for him, and he gradually compromised his love for God to accommodate the wishes of his heathen wives. Statistics from *The New International Dictionary of the Bible* state that the harem of Solomon held a collection of seven hundred wives and three hundred concubines.

The book of Ecclesiastes is a journal-like account of Solomon's life of opulence and power. It is also a book of despair at the personal meaninglessness of his attainments. Read these often-quoted words in the book's opening chapter:

> *"Meaningless! Meaningless!"* . . .
> *"Utterly meaningless!*
> *Everything is meaningless."*
> *What do people gain from all their labors*
> *at which they toil under the sun?*
> *Generations come and generations go,*
> *but the earth remains forever.*
> *The sun rises and the sun sets,*
> *and hurries back to where it rises.*
> *The wind blows to the south*
> *and turns to the north;*

round and round it goes,
ever returning
on its course.
All streams flow into the sea,
yet the sea is never full.
To the place the streams come from,
there they return again.
All things are wearisome,
more than one can say.
The eye never has enough of seeing,
nor the ear its fill of hearing.
What has been will be again.
What has been done will be done again;
there is nothing new under the sun.
Is there anything of which one can say,
"Look! This is something new"?
It was here already, long ago;
it was here before our time.
No one remembers the former generations,
and even those yet to come
will not be remembered
by those who follow them. (vv. 2–11 NIV)

These opening thoughts are followed by a denouncement of everything else humanity generally considers of value: wisdom, pleasure, power, work, sex, and money. "Whoever loves money never has enough; whoever loves wealth is never satisfied with their income. This too is meaningless" (Ecclesiastes 5:10 NIV).

Solomon apparently decided since nothing in his life had meaning, the remedy was to eat, drink, and to find minimal satisfaction during the few days of life God had given him. Then, after eleven chapters of expressing his disillusionment, Solomon seemed to come back to his earlier spiritual moorings. He concluded his thoughts in chapter 12 by saying, "Remember your Creator in the days of your youth" (v. 1 NIV) and "fear God and keep his commandments, for this is the duty of all mankind" (v. 13 NIV).

Possibly Solomon came to agree with his own father's words we quoted earlier: "All our busy rushing ends in nothing. . . . My only hope is in you."

The Gigantic Truth That Gives Meaning

I don't believe it is possible for any of us to find ultimate meaning in life apart from placing our hope in a God who is and who always will be a God who cares about every detail of our lives. That gigantic truth settles us down to trust him and to remember he is the God who sovereignly set everything in motion. The meaning we crave, the meaning for which we search, is the meaning he intends for us to fully experience.

The great Russian writer Leo Tolstoy did not have a

sense of a sovereign, caring God who invited Tolstoy to place his hope in the Creator of all life. Tolstoy came hurtling to that great ache for knowing after he was a famous and very wealthy man. He had written such classics as *War and Peace* and *Anna Karenina*, but in the midst of all his acclaim, the celebrity, wealth, and activities he had been caught up in for years began to disenchant him. He found himself asking about the meaning of it all: *What was life? What was its purpose? What was his purpose?*

Tolstoy's inability to answer those questions horrified him. He came to the conclusion that everything he had done with his life had no value, no merit; it seemed utterly without meaning.

In his *Confessions*, Tolstoy sounds like Solomon in Ecclesiastes:

> My deeds, whatever they may be, will be forgotten sooner or later, and I myself will be no more. Why then do anything? How can anyone fail to see this and live? That's what is amazing! Is it possible to live only as long as life intoxicates us? Once we are sober we cannot help seeing it is all a delusion, a stupid delusion![1]

Tolstoy's anguish led to much soul searching and biblical investigation—and ultimately to a relationship with God. That conversion experience produced an internal peace and assurance that God had designed his life for meaning far beyond what writing, fame, and money could provide.

The Restless Itch for *More*

Why is the search for meaning such a universal craving, and why does despair so often overwhelm the seeker? The answer to those questions can be found in the definition of the word *meaning*. One definition is that it's "something that is felt to be the inner significance of something." If something occupies our time, dictates our dailiness, and provides structure for our very existence, it must have inner significance. Tolstoy's life was structured by his writing, and that writing provided the wealth and fame he loved, so why did all that lose meaning for him? It became meaning-less because there was no inner significance to it all.

Solomon also had to redirect his focus from satisfying his cravings for material things to an understanding of how God provides inner significance. He created all of us with a deep potential to experience a rich inner life, and we crave that for which we were created. Genesis says God breathed into his creation the breath of life (Genesis 2:7), which includes the spirit of life. That God-infused spirit instilled within us gives us the need to live for something beyond our external needs. We were created to live for something other than ourselves. We were created to live for that which benefits others.

Remember, when Jesus was asked what is the most important commandment in Scripture, he said, "You must love the
LORD your God with all your heart, all your soul, and all
your mind. This is the first and greatest commandment. A
second is equally important. 'Love your neighbor as yourself.'
The entire law and all the demands of the prophets are based
on these two commandments" (Matthew 22:36–40).

In these verses recorded by Matthew, Jesus summed
up inner significance, which provides meaning for our
existence. But is it really that simple? Yes, it really is.

The response, for each of us, is first loving God and
then loving others. If we get out of sequence with the pri-
ority that loving God comes first, we can get caught up
in a "good-deeds life" that is merely an extension of our
humanity. We can work tirelessly for the benefit of others
and still miss the meaning intended for us. But when we
do good deeds in the name of God and out of our love for
God, we transcend ourselves. Our motivation is then God-
focused. *He* is our inner significance that provides meaning
for all we do.

I have a dear friend who finds pleasurable meaning in
knitting. She was at one time a principal of an elementary
school in Garden Grove, California, and she was a mentor
to me as a first-year teacher. I struggled that year because
I was assigned to teach third grade instead of high school
English. My third graders were adorable, but I was more

prepared to teach Shakespeare than reading fundamentals. My mentor and soon-to-become friend walked me through the process of changing my mental images and remembering that I had indeed done a semester of practice teaching with third graders in preparation for my degree in education. I learned to love those squirmy little kids and even rose to the challenge of improving their reading skills. I owe that accomplishment to the patience and wisdom of my mentor.

Due to a series of severe medical challenges, my mentor-friend has been confined to her home for years. This woman who once found meaning in her work as a brilliant educator and administrator now finds meaning in knitting baby blankets, sweaters, and anything else that requires the clicking of needles.

Residents in homes for unwed mothers as well as shelters providing safety for abused women and children have all found comfort, warmth, and beauty in the work of my friend's hands. She is loving her neighbors and finding meaning and inner significance in spite of medical challenges.

Perhaps there are a few of you who do not identify with my mentor friend. You may be more like Beckett's characters Vladimir and Estragon, who are waiting for Godot. You don't like the wait, don't understand why you wait, and are not even sure who you're waiting for. You simply know there's got to be meaning in something somewhere, and you don't want to miss it. Tolstoy didn't want to miss it either. He was convinced that life's meaning would come as he became increasingly famous and wealthy. Instead, he felt confused and empty, still craving something beyond his reach.

Solomon might tell Tolstoy, Vladimir, Estragon, and anyone else searching for meaning in life to give it up . . . life has no meaning. But Jesus refutes all those despairing thoughts with these words: "I am the way, the truth and the life," and "I have come that they may have life and that they may have it more abundantly" (John 14:6; 10:10 NKJV).

The abundant life Christ offers us relieves us of uncertainty, searching, and despair. The abundant life is resting in the peace of God's bigger-than-life love.

Ten

FINDING *MORE* IN GOD'S PURPOSE FOR OUR LIVES

I'VE NEVER HAD A PERSONAL CONVERSATION THAT BEGAN WITH someone asking me, "Marilyn, what is your favorite insect?"

Instead most conversations begin with such queries as, "How are you? What's new in your life . . . how's your hammertoe?"

I have a ready answer for the insect question in the event it is ever asked. "Yes, I have a very, very favorite insect: the ladybug."

Ladybugs have pleased my soul since childhood. They seem so cheerful, so innocent, so colorful, so busy. Recently I've been thrilled to discover an even more meaningful descriptor for ladybugs: they are purposeful. In addition to providing me with pleasure, ladybugs have a job to do, and they eagerly get at it at every opportunity.

What is their purpose? It is to eat up the mean-spirited insects that prey upon my flowers. The ladybug's specialty is aphids, a particularly insidious invader. One ladybug can eat as many as five thousand aphids in a lifetime. I say that accomplishment deserves some recognition, perhaps a lifetime achievement award!

Two weeks ago I renewed my love of and commitment to these little warriors who courageously (or perhaps just hungrily) battle the enemies of my defenseless flower garden. Kipp, my landscaper, brought me two mesh pouches full of live, eager little ladybugs. My instructions were to water the flowers at dusk and then release the ladies from their pouches. They would instantly crawl into the flowerpots and begin banqueting. That sounded simple enough. Unfortunately, however, I needed to leave my house that afternoon too early to follow Kipp's dusk-water-release instructions. I had to meet my friends for an outing we had planned, and that meant leaving home before dusk.

Prior to leaving I peered into the pouches and wondered if the ladies would die due to my before-dusk social life. How long could they survive in their crowded pouches?

I enjoyed being with my friends but was preoccupied all evening with the well-being of the "girls," so when I got home that night, after dark, I cut one of the pouches open and released the ladies into three of my pots. I could not really see what was going on with them but hoped for the best. Maybe they didn't realize dusk had come and gone.

I needed a safe, cool place for the remaining pouch-house and decided my shower floor would be perfect. I settled their pouches there, and then, feeling I was tending to their security fairly well, I went to bed.

The next morning, when I walked into the bathroom, I

was stunned to see the shower walls crawling with ladybugs! I stared mindlessly at the swarm, wondering, *What . . . how could this happen?*

Gingerly reaching for the pouch-house, I saw that a corner of the pouch had been cut open. *Drat.* I must have partially cut the pouch when I cut the other one in the dark. *That's what happens, Marilyn, when you alter the rules to accommodate your wild and wooly social life: the ladies in your care escape into a world of utter chaos and meaninglessness.*

The poor, befuddled ladies were experiencing meaninglessness because there were no aphids lurking about my shower walls; there were no insects whose evil intent is the destruction of the flowers in my porch pots. The ladies were frantically crawling around aimlessly, unable to fulfill the purpose for which they were created. They appeared confused and utterly bewildered, and I was stricken with guilt.

I carefully scooped, encouraged, and compelled one hundred or so of the ladies to crawl to safety in a huge ziplock bag I held open with one hand while herding the bugs with the other. Then, at 9:00 a.m., I released them to the pots to fulfill their lives' purpose. It was early morning, not dusk, and I fretted for hours.

Kipp came over later in the day, and I made my confession to him. I'm sure there are rules that say no priest is supposed to laugh hysterically over the sin of the penitent, but Kipp did. He laughed while assuring me the ladies had undoubtedly found what they were looking for in my flower-pots; he told me to lighten up and then drove way, collapsed over his steering wheel in a new round of hysterics.

Acknowledging Our Purpose for Living

In case you're wondering, I have a purpose for telling you about my ladybugs. All created creatures—from the ladybug to you, reading this book—have a God-given purpose for living. In the last chapter we talked about God-given meaning for living and how the craving and searching imperative for all of us is to determine life's meaning. Our meaning comes not from an accumulation of earthly fame, power, or money but from a spiritual and personal acknowledgment of God. He created us for a relationship with him, service to him and to others.

So then, let's consider our purpose for living. The distinction between *meaning* and *purpose* is helpful because they serve very different but defining functions for us. When I finally discover the meaning of my life, I'm not meant to sit by the side of the road content with my discovery. The God-given meaning for life comes with the desire for purpose in life. *Meaning* is about being; *purpose* is about doing. What are we supposed to *do*? What is the God-given purpose for our existence?

Trying to consider these heady questions, it would be

much easier to be a ladybug. They don't have options; they are created for one purpose. But human beings have many possible options. To begin with, our first purpose is to love and serve God, but there are usually a number of different options we can choose that will express that purpose.

For example, my purpose has been lived out through four different options: teacher, counselor, speaker, and writer. These are my professional purposes, and all fall within the range of my giftedness. But because I have a narrow band of competence, were I to stray from those purposes, disaster would ensue. I could not be a bus driver because, though I like to drive, I often lose track of where I am. *Am I supposed to be in Idaho? When did I leave Texas?* I could not be a nurse, though I have compassion. I would forget who gets what medication and on what schedule. I could not work for the IRS because I can't figure out what I owe or why; I could never make that mystifying procedure comprehensible. (Can anyone?)

Many of us have chosen to be a wife, husband, and parent in addition to other professional options. Some choose to do both at the same time. I chose to be a wife and mother; only later in the lives of my children did I add the professional expressions of my purpose. All these roles have equal meaning and purpose; with each of them is the call to serve God and others.

Much of knowing our purpose in life is knowing our individual strengths and then living out of those strengths.

When we recognize that our gifts are sovereignly designed and placed within us for a specific divine purpose, our life track is clarified. I have rarely questioned my life purpose but have often wondered where and how I was meant to live it out. We'll talk later about that "where and how."

While my focus here is on looking to God for our purpose, I must also acknowledge that those who do not look to God for purpose, those who feel no imperative to love and serve him, can still live a life of clearly defined purpose that is of enormous value to the community. My grandfather was a man of integrity, compassion, and deep commitment to the needs of others. He had no faith or belief in the God of the Bible. But my grandfather's drive to make the world a better place never wavered. That drive had its origin in the mind of a man who felt no need of a personal god nor ever sought to find him. His god was bettering the world through good deeds.

As a lawyer and municipal judge in the state of Colorado, my grandfather was often an intercessor for oppressed and disenfranchised persons who sought representation from someone who would do for them what they could not do for themselves. For him, that was his life's purpose. The irony was that Jesus did for my grandfather what Grandfather did for others. When my grandfather died of a heart attack at age sixty-four, he left a rich and meaningful earthly heritage. But there could have been more for him, so much more.

The How, When, and Where of
Living Out Our Purpose

Since the meaning of life is knowing and loving God followed by loving others, our purpose is narrowed down to
our understanding of our gifts and how, when, or where
God means to use them. For my grandfather, that was not
an issue. He utilized his gifts how, when, and where he
chose to use them. But as Christ followers, we seek to find
divine guidance for how, when, and where. And that, unfortunately, can create stress and uncertainty in our souls.

How do we know God's will for living out our purpose?
We ask him, of course. But discerning his answer is sometimes challenging. If only God spoke out loud today as he
did in the Old Testament; it would be so much easier to
know his will.

At one time my life questions would have been: *How do
I know the difference between my voice and God's voice in my heart
and my mind? How do I know it's my will or his will to teach in
California or in Washington?* After Ken died, *How am I to know
if I am supposed to sell our house?* And later, I would have asked,
*Is it God's will for me to sell my condo in California and buy that
house in Texas? Is it God's will that I leave the state of my birth and
move to a part of Texas where there are no sandy ocean beaches?*

My inevitable and frequently asked question throughout these stages of my life was, *God, what do you think?*

Jesus gave one very specific answer to that question in his Sermon on the Mount:

Therefore I say to you, do not worry about your life, what you will eat or what you will drink; nor about your body, what you will put on. . . .

Which of you by worrying can add one cubit to his stature? . . .

But seek first the kingdom of God and His righteousness, and all these things shall be added to you. Therefore do not worry about tomorrow. (Matthew 6:25, 27, 33–34 NKJV)

So one thing we know about God's will is we are not to worry about the future. Jesus said that being anxious shows a lack of trust in God's provision for us in the present as well as the future. But what do we do then with the how, when, or where issues?

Is it possible that we make knowing the how, when, or where of God's will a bigger issue for us than he intends it to be? God's Holy Spirit–infused book does not tell me where to live. Instead it tells me *how* to live. When I know how to live, and I commit to it, that kind of living can occur in California, Washington, Texas, or Africa. His purpose and my purpose can link in that common goal of loving him and loving others anywhere on the planet.

God is not indifferent to the details of my life, however. In fact, he is totally in control of the details of my life. That's why it is possible for the Christ follower to relax and not worry about the now or the future. And yes, it is possible that we make knowing the how, when, or where of God's will a bigger issue for us than he intends it to be. It is true his purpose for us of loving him and loving others can occur anywhere on the planet, but the amazing truth is, he has a specific how, when, and where for it all.

Why am I so sure? Ephesians 1:11 includes the phrase "being predestined according to the purpose of Him who works all things according to the counsel of His will" (NKJV). For thirty years that verse has been my guiding cloud by day and pillar of fire by night, leading me through life the way God led the Israelites through the wilderness.

The End of Anxiety

Until I learned more about the sovereign design of God's plan for my life and purpose, I tended to be anxious. *What if I messed up my life by making wrong decisions? What if I didn't pray enough? What if I didn't have ears to hear or eyes to see?* These conscientious questions could at times be agonizing.

But my anxiety ultimately diminished as I studied God's Word and absorbed verses like these:

I know, LORD, that our lives are not our own. We are not able to plan our own course. (Jeremiah 10:23)

You can make many plans, but the LORD's purpose will prevail. (Proverbs 19:21)

These verses are foundational to an understanding of God's sovereign design for my purpose in life. In it all, God invites my participation in planning, evaluating, and ultimately choosing the options that appear to make sense to me. The safety net is simply that I participate, but I'm not in charge. He's in charge of everything concerning my options.

So I can stop being anxious, trusting that God knows exactly how he intends to "grow me up" as well as how he will use me for his purposes. So when I make a plan and the door closes on it, I'm reminded, "the LORD's purpose will prevail."

I'm also reminded of another peace-producing truth in Romans 8:26–28:

The Holy Spirit prays for us with groanings that cannot be expressed in words. And the Father who knows all hearts knows what the Sprit is saying, for the Spirit pleads for us believers in harmony with God's own will. And we know that God causes everything to work together for the good of those who love God and are called according to his purpose for them.

Understanding these truths affirming God's sovereignty over our purposes lets us stop the magical thinking that sometimes springs up in our heads as we attempt to know his will.

- *That check came in the mail the very day I was wondering if I should buy a new house. Could it be a sign?*
- *He got sick the very day we were supposed to fly to Florida. Could it be a sign?*

I want always to look to Scripture instead of to signs, which may be no more than human assumptions and hopes that add fuel to a fire not meant to be.

Proverbs 3:6 says, "Seek his will in all you do, and he will show you which path to take."

We can count on the fact that we can count on him.

Clarifying Your Sense of Purpose

Just in case your sense of purpose needs clarification, perhaps the following suggestions may be helpful:

- Do a study on your strengths. I highly recommend the book *Find Your Strongest Life* by Marcus Buckingham as a resource for guiding you through this study.

- Recognize that those strengths have been given to you for the purpose of serving God and others.

- Thank God for his plan for you as well as for the how and where that plan unfolds every day.

- Release your need to control all things, and commit to giving God control of all things. You will know you have released your need to control when you find yourself worrying less.

- Rest in the reassurance of Psalm 32:8: "I will guide you along the best pathway for your life."

- Remember you are held tenderly by your Father's hand; he will never let you go. He knows you and calls you by name.

The One Answer to Our Constant Craving

There is only one answer to our craving for more meaning or more purpose in life, and that is God himself. His love, participation, and direction in all we do come not from a dictator but from a father. He is a father who takes pleasure in his children, watches over their activities, and determines when is just the right time for their next step. If there is a misstep, he goes after us and places us back on the path of his choosing.

Like any good father, he provides security. He knows we can be "as frail as breath" (Isaiah 2:22). And he promises that we find "shelter in the shadow of [his] wings" (Psalm 36:7).

Eleven

FINDING MORE
MEANING IN SOLITUDE

MANY PEOPLE HAVE A CRAVING FOR MORE SOLITUDE THAN THEY are able to experience in their demanding and hurried lives. Mothers of young children are among those who sometimes feel that craving, which can send them retreating to the bathroom to lock the door and simply luxuriate in privacy for a few quiet moments. Those moments may not last long, however, as soon little fingers curl under the door and plaintive cries of "Mama, come out" become too persistent to ignore.

Each of us has her own threshold of overdosing on social interaction and togetherness. We can reach a point where we've had our fill of human contact. That can come after an especially hectic workday, a week of houseguests, or increased socializing during the holidays. Those times may create a deep inner craving within us to go off and be alone. That aloneness does not mean we wish to be cut off indefinitely from human contact. We may simply need to refuel, recharge, and replenish our interior beings in order to live our lives with enthusiasm and energy.

Seeking that kind of solitude, my father took two years off from the ministry and purchased forty acres of remote farmland in Washington state. My parents appropriately named that property "Lonely Acres." I've written about that experience before, but I want to share yet another facet of it in this discussion on solitude.

Dad was suffering from "clergy burnout" that threatened his emotional and physical well-being. Raising hybrid blueberries and strawberries was a boon to his soul; so were the two cows, six chickens, one rooster, and a pig. For my dad, taking time out from pastoral duties and sinking into that two-year period of solitude was not a luxury; it was as much a necessity for him as food, water, and oxygen.

During that time Dad reexamined what God's purpose was for his life. *Had he really been called to the ministry? Did he have the emotional and physical stamina for the job? Why was he experiencing burnout?* He mulled these questions around in his mind and spirit as he plowed an acre of land with a borrowed tractor and planted alfalfa.

He wondered if God's purpose was for him to return to the soil and farm as his father had. Maybe he had misunderstood God's leading and needed to experience burnout to realize he was not living out God's purpose after all. These were sobering issues to contemplate.

But those two years were ultimately restorative to his mind, body, and soul. One day as he was hoeing his strawberry field, he sensed the unmistakable presence of God and the inner assurance that he had not only called Dad to the ministry but that it was also time to return. Within three months Dad sold Lonely Acres at an enormous profit and resumed pastoring. He never again doubted his God-given purpose, and he pastored until his retirement many years later.

Restorative, Meaningful Solitude

So what was that all about? God in his nurturing love provided a time of reflection and solitude for my dad. With that restorative solitude came the assurance of God's call on Dad's life as well as the need to replenish his mind and body with physical labor. God's plan was being accomplished.

I believe God's plan is always accomplished and he "works all things according to the counsel of His will" (Ephesians 1:11). We often don't "get" what God is doing and why. But that's okay. He knows; I trust that—except, of course, for those times when my humanity kicks up and I fuss and get cranky. When that occurs, I need solitude to do its work as I pray myself back to what Scripture says. Remember Proverbs 19:21? "You can make many plans, but the LORD's purpose will prevail."

God's purpose for my dad was ultimately made known to him as God and solitude worked together. An interesting fact about solitude is that a person may be in a state of stillness and quiet but not be lonely in that solitary state. Solitude is often characterized by active contemplation; that's how it worked for my dad. However, for me at age ten, the two-year farm period produced loneliness without the positive effects of solitude. When we feel lonely we may feel an isolation that can lead to despair. Solitude can be productive. Loneliness can be destructive.

I dealt with my loneliness in a variety of ways. Since there were no kids living anywhere near me, books became my best friends. A "bookmobile" (a library on wheels) stopped at the end of Williams Road every two weeks. That was a bike trip of a mile and a half. I rigged up a box that attached to my bike and pedaled eagerly to the bookmobile to exchange my books for new ones. Then I'd pedal home, scramble up into the tree house I'd built, and read until dinnertime.

This reading was not a time of solitude, however, but of diversion. The books kept me from feeling what was going on inside me. I felt isolated, and I didn't like that feeling, so I read to counteract my emotions.

One day Mother asked me about a particular book she noticed I kept renewing. It was entitled *Sawdust in His Shoes*. She asked me what the book was about and why I was repeatedly reading it. I told her the book was about a little boy who dreamed of running away and joining a circus. Ultimately he did run away, and the circus people let him feed the elephants. He traveled everywhere with the circus and loved it more than anything he could ever have imagined.

My mother looked at me and tenderly asked, "Do you want to run away, honey?"

That question opened the floodgates for me. I had not realized I wanted to run away, but as I sank into my mother's arms and sobbed, I knew why I kept reading *Sawdust in His Shoes*.

She told me she, too, was lonely living "way out here away from civilization" and that she understood how I might want to run away. But she told me everything in life has a beginning, middle, and an end. "There will be an end to living here, honey, because I know your daddy is called to the ministry. God is going to make that known in his own time."

I was stunned to realize my mother was feeling some of *my* feelings. I was comforted by her words reassuring me that circumstances have a beginning, middle, and end. It made me believe I could wait if I had to. I also felt encouraged to know God was not done with my daddy. I decided God hadn't lost track of any of us.

Mother also suggested that how we think can affect how we feel. We decided to make a game about how many things in a day we could change from a bad feeling to a good thought. We each kept our own daily list and compared our lists at bedtime. This "game" was enormously comforting to me and laid new brain tracks for me to use as I processed each day. I continue to use this game as I interpret the events of my life.

My father craved solitude in order to clarify his inner world and be assured it was a fit with his external world. As a child I only knew that his solitude became my loneliness. As an adult I've come to realize that the introspection of solitude does not necessarily produce loneliness. Instead, solitude can be a means of achieving optimal mental health.

Cultivating a Craving for Solitude

Just in case you do not crave more solitude, may I suggest it is a craving we all might want to cultivate. I tend to crave more people than more solitude. Part of that preference is due to my personality type. People have always energized me and I love being wherever I can find them. But I understand the benefits of solitude; so perhaps we need reminders about those benefits and how we might do a bit more retreating into the richness of our inner selves.

There are many ways to experience the benefits of solitude; one of my favorites has always been walking. When Ken and I lived in Laguna Beach, California, one of our favorite morning activities was a thirty-minute walk along the ocean's edge, a walk that led ultimately to Scandia

Bakery (a route that required a sharp right turn and no willpower).

That routine delighted me because of Ken's presence as well as an apple turnover; we walked, talked, and ate. But Ken needed something different, and although he enjoyed the walking, talking, and eating, he craved a daily time of meaningful solitude. Though it really was not my preference, we agreed that it would benefit us both if we walked alone (and avoided that sharp right turn leading to Scandia Bakery). Ken needed time to think; I reluctantly decided I did too.

As we went our separate ways each morning, I was reminded that walking alone causes me to concentrate on my own thoughts and not those of whomever I may be walking with. Walking in solitude can be a problem-solving time when I think through circumstances that need attention, emotions that are troubling, or search for solutions that have eluded me. Perhaps the greatest value for walking alone is that I become aware of the necessity to pay more attention to my inner need to absorb Jesus. That leads me to another beneficial experience of solitude: meditation.

Meditating in Solitude

During that time of living in Laguna Beach, I had a favorite rock in a cove not too far from our house. I would either sit in the sand or on the rock and just let my mind slip into neutral. My focal point was quietly saying the name of Jesus. The more I said his name, the more focused I became on only him. Even the roar of the waves, the blue sky, and the fussing of the seagulls receded into the background. I was there with Jesus. He was outside, inside, and throughout my entire being.

Living now in Frisco, Texas, I have a sweet meditation time I call "Jesus, tea, and me." I have a patio that houses my favorite flowers in their pots. There in my favorite Brown Jordan chair, I'm nurtured by the sounds of the lake fountain and the singing of Texan birds as I sit sipping my tea and murmuring, "Jesus, Jesus, Jesus."

Another solitary experience that feeds and centers my soul is praying out loud. I've been a widow for twenty-one years, and my habit of praying out loud is reason enough not to consider remarrying. I might be able to give up my house for his but not my need to pray out loud. I've never been good at kneeling and praying. Neither do I sit and pray well. But as I move through the house, up the stairs, down the stairs, do the laundry, and brew my tea, my thoughts come tumbling out to Jesus.

Not only do I pray out loud in every room of the house, I pray out loud when I drive. I bought a new car last year with a great sound system, but I rarely turn it on. It competes with the sound of my voice. I love the fact so many people are now driving alone and talking on their hands-free cell phones. It makes me blend in more easily; I no longer create suspicion from other drivers as they see me, alone in my car, gesturing and talking animatedly.

The value of praying out loud is that I often do not know what I think until I hear myself saying it. Often my words do not seem to be preceded by tangible thoughts. When I start telling Jesus what I didn't know until I said it, I have to then ask him, "What do you think about what I just said?"

These tumbling statements become more organized and create a mental clarity I didn't have before I said them.

An unbeliever friend once said to me, "Well, Marilyn, you would get the same mental clarity by just standing in front of a tree and blurting out your thoughts. Why do you call what you do praying to God?"

My response was, "For one thing, I'm talking to the One who made the tree. And in addition to that, the tree can't hear me and doesn't love me—or even know me!"

My time to hear God's responses to my praying out loud often comes in my spirit as I meditate. And certainly his responses are evident when I read his Word. For example, when I asked him what he thought about me moving from California to Texas, he spoke to me through Psalm 48:14: "For this is God, Our God forever and ever; He will be our guide even to death" (NKJV).

I understood that verse as a reminder that he would guide me in beginning my new life in Texas.

Created for Connection

These are the positive contributions of solitude for establishing and maintaining optimal mental and spiritual health. But as we've discussed, solitude is not always viewed as beneficial. When solitude is thrust upon us against our wishes, we can experience the despair of isolation; we were created for connection.

One of the most dreaded punishments in the penal system is solitary confinement. It taps into a fundamental fear of humankind dating perhaps from earliest infancy, when every human being is totally dependent upon and at the mercy of persons much more powerful than the helpless infant. This kind of prison isolation can produce depression, confusion, and often hallucinations.

For the person who brings a well-furnished mind to solitary confinement, however, there are dramatic stories of maintaining emotional centeredness. The noted violinist Yehudi Menuhin told the story of Antal Dorati, the mother of his conductor. At the end of the war, when the Germans were rounding up the Jews in Budapest, she was one of the few who did not lose her sanity. She remained sane by methodically going through the four parts of each of the Beethoven quartets, which she knew individually by heart.

Russian writer Dostoevsky spent eight years in solitary confinement charged with crimes against the state. As a political prisoner he was not allowed books or writing materials. Ultimately he was given a notebook in which he recorded the phrases and expressions used by fellow convicts. Its contents were used in *House of the Dead* and published after his release. Writing helped refocus his mind from living in prison to mentally writing books and short stories.

There are many who testify that when solitary confinement is given personal meaning, there is the mental capacity to more easily survive the experience. As we have discussed in previous chapters, it is mandatory that we have a clear sense of meaning and purpose in our lives for all times and in all places—including those times when we might prefer to be with others but find ourselves alone.

One of the most inspiring biographies I have ever read is Eric Metaxas's *Bonhoeffer*. As a pastor and writer, Bonhoeffer became increasingly alarmed by the rise of the Nazi regime in his beloved Germany. He realized Hitler's evil powers were not only a threat to the life of Germany but to all of Europe. Bonhoeffer then determined Hitler had to be fought against and defeated in any way possible.

When he learned of Bonhoeffer's influence, passion,

and zeal, Hitler sentenced him to solitary confinement at Buchenwald, famous as one of the Nazi centers of death. Hitler personally gave the orders for Bonhoeffer's execution a short time later. Before he died, Bonhoeffer wrote these words: "Silence in the face of evil is itself evil: God will not hold us guiltless. Not to speak is to speak. Not to act is to act."

Solitude serves many beneficial purposes. Sometimes we simply need to draw back, regroup, and then rejoin the rhythm of our lives. Always we need the solitude that provides spiritual communion with God. And on those rare occasions where we may be called to be heroic for him in places of enforced solitude, we remember a well-furnished mind houses God's promises to us:

The LORD himself goes before you and will be with you; he will never leave you nor forsake you. Do not be afraid; do not be discouraged. (Deuteronomy 31:8 NIV)

For the LORD loves the just and will not forsake his faithful ones. They will be protected forever. (Psalm 37:28 NIV)

For I am the LORD your God, who takes hold of your right hand and says to you, Do not fear; I will help you. (Isaiah 41:13 NIV)

I will lead the blind by ways they have not known, along unfamiliar paths I will guide them; I will turn the darkness into light before them; and make the rough places smooth. These are the things I will do; I will not forsake them. (Isaiah 42:16 NIV)

Twelve

FINDING FREEDOM
FROM THE CRAVING
FOR REVENGE

AT THE AGE OF SIX I ANNOUNCED TO MY STARTLED PARENTS THAT I was living under oppression. Working to control the grin muscles in his face, Dad said, "What do you mean by oppression? In what way are you being oppressed?"

I said, "I am the only one in the neighborhood who has to go to bed by seven. It's embarrassing; I hate going to bed before it's even dark outside."

"Well, honey," Dad said, "you seem to feel strongly about that; anything else we should know?"

"Yes, there's one more thing," I continued. "I am the only kid in the neighborhood who does not get an allowance. I never have any money of my own, and I feel really poor."

My mother, though compassionate about my sense of oppression, asked with a note of pride, "Marilyn, how do you happen to know the word *oppression*?"

It always pleased me to play into her love of words by tossing out a few of my own. I explained that I learned about oppression in Sunday school from a story about people who were slaves in Egypt. They had to make bricks from mud and straw and were never paid. But Moses got them out of there and took them to a great place where they got paid.

I must have presented a convincing case because I got a list of jobs I could do for which I was paid. And my bed-time was changed from seven to eight o'clock. In all this I learned a new word: *negotiation.* My father pointed out to me that slaves were not able to negotiate, so I really was not at all like the people Moses had to get out of Egypt.

When I became a "salaried" member of my kid-society and personal dignity was restored by no longer having to be in bed by seven, I lost interest in the topic of oppression. The awareness of Israelite slavery in Egypt became a dis-tant memory. I had been set free!

Interestingly, as a six-year-old kid I reenacted the themes of a human drama that is thousands of years old. History is replete with accounts of civilizations living under tyranni-cal leaders oppressing people who were seemingly powerless to change their circumstances and suffered enormously as a result.

To infer that I was living under a tyrannical regime is absurd. Nevertheless, I felt the need to change my circum-stances, and that was possible only by talking to those in control of those circumstances. Because caring and benev-olent parents governed my environment, my concerns were heard and acted upon.

Let's flash back to the Israelite slaves who had been the

source of my inspiration. They suffered heartless and inhumane treatment from their Egyptian captors. Beaten with metal-tipped whips, deprived of sleep, food, and water, those who could not endure were kicked aside and left to die. Their circumstances were unendurable. They needed someone to help them by talking to those in control of their circumstances. They needed a negotiator or, better yet, a mediator. The God who cared and saw it all appointed Moses to be that mediator. His job was to represent the needs of God's people as well as the will of God to Pharaoh.

God's message to Pharaoh through Moses was, "Let my people go."

If you are well schooled in Scripture, you will remember the relentless drama that occurred before a defeated and miracle-weary Pharaoh finally released the Israelites to Moses. They left on their journey to the land God had promised through Abraham centuries earlier.

You may also remember that forty-year journey was not an easy trip, especially for Moses, who had served as an able mediator with Pharaoh. One would think when the Israelites were released to ultimately claim the land God had promised them, their oppression would be over. It wasn't.

Oppression is defined as a feeling of being heavily weighed down, either mentally or physically. There is no doubt that slavery in Egypt was an unendurable experience that weighed down the Israelites both mentally and physically; there is no question they were *oppressed*. Their feelings in Egypt were understandable, but was there a reasonable explanation for those feelings to continue after they were set free? They were no longer slaves and no longer abused. So what was their problem?

Understanding Freedom, a State of Being

Freedom is defined as being free of restraints, having the capacity to exercise choice and to do as one wishes. Unlike oppression, freedom is not a feeling; it is a state of being. The Israelites thought life would become positive, happy, and carefree once their freedom was secured. They would have the ongoing pleasure of envisioning the perfection of the promised land. But instead they had to walk endlessly in the hot desert and eat manna for every single meal day after day. The monotony began to weigh them down mentally; they lapsed into the familiar feeling of oppression. They did not feel free.

This time, however, they didn't fear their slave overseers and ultimately Pharaoh; they didn't have to hide their feelings. They complained and whined to Moses and behaved like children until Moses desperately pleaded their case to God. The Israelites were sick of manna; they were craving meat. God satisfied their craving by sending low-flying quail all around their camp. Now they had more meat than they could possible consume. Did their feeling of oppression subside? Yes, until they got sick of quail.

In deference to the Israelites and their insatiable cravings, I did try to negotiate an increase in my allowance shortly after receiving it. I thought negotiating had gone so well the first time, I'd give it another try. My father was unmoved. I left the negotiating table with my fixed income and was encouraged to appreciate what I had. (I showed early signs of wanting more.)

Freedom is more than a safe environment where we have opportunities to exercise our free will and to make choices. Freedom is not a feeling. Freedom is a fact, a state of being. In contrast, oppression is a feeling that distorts our freedom by focusing not on what *is* but on what is still being craved. When our cravings get the best of us, we become imprisoned by them; like the Israelites, we don't feel free.

God called the prophet Isaiah to "bring good news to the poor. He has sent me to comfort the brokenhearted and to proclaim that captives will be released and prisoners will be freed" (Isaiah 61:1). This is not only a promise for external freedom but also for internal freedom. Isaiah states God's desire is "to set the oppressed free and break every yoke" (Isaiah 58:6 NIV).

It is far easier for us to understand freedom in the context of our external world than our internal state. Human beings have engaged in wars since the beginning of civilization.

Most often, humanity's motivation has been to experience freedom from political oppression. But when God says he wants the oppressed set free and he wants to "break every yoke," he is also talking about emotional freedom.

The Craving for Revenge

The word *yoke* produces a powerful image; a yoke is a crossbar designed to be carried across a person's shoulders with equal loads suspended from each end. The question we might ask ourselves is, *What is the load we are carrying on our personal crossbar?*

One of the heaviest loads many of us carry is an unforgiving spirit toward those who have hurt us. The oppression we experience from unforgiveness is an enormous challenge; it becomes a yoke that assures us of continued captivity. We all know we need to forgive, but many of us have no motivation to forgive. Why? Quite simply, we feel the person who hurt us does not deserve forgiveness.

Surely all of us have been the object of a behavior we feel is unforgivable. It may have been a slanderous lie that undermined our integrity, ruined our reputation, or even cost us our job. It may have been the infidelity of a spouse who wrongly blamed us for everything and got custody of the kids. It may have been the sexual exploitation of a father, brother, uncle, grandfather, or other person who counted our trust and virginity as nothing of value. We could go on and on listing the enormous possibilities of hurt and pain experienced by others.

In such cases we wonder if some behaviors are so bad there is no forgiveness for them. On our human scale of justice, we sometimes decide who should be forgiven and who should not. We may feel the person or persons who wronged us should somehow have to pay for what they did. And it is here, in this place of oppression, that we experience a new craving: *revenge.*

I had never felt deeply about getting revenge for anything until our then seventeen-year-old daughter, Beth, a virgin, was date-raped. For the first time in my life, I had murderous thoughts that, though frightening in their intensity, felt perfectly justifiable. I believed that the man, ten years older than Beth, had no right to live, breathe, or walk the earth again. To make the offense even worse, she became pregnant.

Both Ken and our son, Jeff, went to the guy's apartment. Ken told him we were going to press charges since Beth was a minor and that since the rape produced a pregnancy, he would be responsible to pay child support. The man seemed contrite but confused. He was from a culture where women's rights were not of paramount importance. Ken had done some research and found that the man didn't have a green card and was working in the country illegally.

I don't know what other conversation took place in that encounter, but to my amazement a week later the guy came to our house, stood on our front porch, and asked forgiveness from me and from Beth. We never saw or heard from him again. Three weeks later Beth miscarried and lost the baby.

What happened to my craving for revenge? Did his seemingly sincere apology settle me down and put my murderous inclinations to rest? Not totally. The sense of injustice for my daughter was slow to dissipate. I carried it in my crossbar longer than was healthy for me.

February 2009 provided the most startling and dramatic lessons of forgiveness and its resulting freedom from oppression when my Women of Faith buddies Lisa Whelchel, Mary Graham, Luci Swindoll, and I went to Rwanda, Africa. We were there to experience the work of World Vision as that organization ministered to a population of people brutalized by the effects of the horrific genocide that occurred in 1995.

To fully grasp the enormity of this event and its effect upon the people, I need to share some of the history of the tribal war between the Tutsi minority and the Hutu-led government of Rwanda. The Tutsi tribe lost its bid for political supremacy during the Hutu revolution of 1959, and as a result the Tutsi tribe was denied the right to live in their homeland. This denial of Tutsi rights resulted in yet another civil war. In 1994, over a period of one hundred days, two million out of seven million people were massacred. Three million people fled the country and lived or died in refugee camps. By the end of July 1994, the genocide had officially halted, but revenge killings continued against the Hutus.

On one of the afternoons during our time in Rwanda, we were driven to the Murambi Genocide Memorial. In room after room on white tables were literally stacks of skulls and grotesque skeletons still in the position in which they died. Although the skeletons were sprinkled with lye, the smell was overwhelming.

In an adjacent room were mountains of clothes removed from the victims as they fled. In yet another display were piles of shoes—shoes of men, women, and children. As I slowly walked through these rooms of hate-inspired slaughter, I felt as if I were in an anteroom of hell. How could the craving for revenge inspire such brutal and inhumane behavior?

I wondered how it was possible for the survivors of this brutal time to continue living, given what they had endured. How would they ever feel hope or trust in another human being again? At dinner that night I got the beginning of the answer to my question. I say the beginning of the answer because I couldn't immediately wrap my mind around its entirety.

A Living Lesson in Forgiveness

A lovely Rwandan woman named Chantal Nyirarukando, who works with World Vision, shared her personal genocide story at the conclusion of our meal. She was married to a Hutu government official. They and Chantal's mother lived in the capital city of Kigali. One afternoon Tutsi rebels stormed into their house, murdering Chantal's mother as well as her husband.

Chantal was not at home but soon became aware of the Hutu slaughter all over the city. Although she was pregnant she managed to flee into the woods. She had to keep running because there was no safety anywhere from the marauding soldiers. After weeks of running and hiding, surviving on grass, berries, and water from a stream, she delivered her own baby. She and the baby survived and were able to return to Kigali after the genocide was over. Now, more than a decade later, she is married to a pastor and expecting their first child together.

I stared in disbelief listening to this story of survival, but I was even more stunned to learn of the ministry Chantal and her husband operate. They are teaching Hutu survivors how to forgive the Tutsis for their brutality that caused near extinction of the entire Hutu tribe. Each week Chantal goes to the jail and visits the Tutsi man who murdered her mother. She not only has forgiven him, she has led him to an understanding of what Christ did on the cross in dying for the sins of the world. This man could not believe Chantal had forgiven him but was even more amazed to realize that God had forgiven him as well.

This message of forgiveness and reconciliation soon began sweeping across Rwanda as people realized that their bitterness and their craving for revenge was costing them their own freedom. Pastors and other Christian leaders are teaching people how to see those who hurt them not as beasts and demons but as human beings who need the power of God to transform their hearts.

Chantal told us one of the greatest challenges in her Christian experience came as she realized she had to ask her mother's murderer to forgive *her* for hating him. Her message to us that evening was that we cannot fully live our lives in communion with each other and with God without the ability to grant and receive forgiveness.

We were all sobered as we walked back to our rooms in the village of Butare. Actually, I felt a bit rebellious. Putting myself in Chantal's place, I could possibly understand the need to forgive those who slaughtered my loved ones, at least in theory, but I wasn't sure I'd actually be able to *do* it. I could maybe point them to Jesus, who by his own atrocious death on the cross could forgive their atrocious sins against their fellow human beings. By bringing that message to them, I probably would feel I had done my part; receiving him or not was their part.

But it was quite another thing to imagine myself forgiving them and then asking that they in turn forgive me. That blew my mind. How could justice be served by my request for forgiveness? They were the murderers who needed to pay the penalty for their heinous crimes.

As we walked I fell into step with Chantal and bluntly said, "I'm impressed you could forgive the man who murdered your mother, but I can't fathom why you needed to ask his forgiveness. Why did you do that?"

Then she told me about the plan she had carried in her mind for months after she discovered which jail housed her mother's murderer. She told me her plan was to get access to his cell, take time to win his confidence—and then kill him. She'd kill him right there in his cell! I was shocked.

Chantal said the change in her plan came as God forcefully caused her to realize that, were she to murder her mother's killer, that act of revenge would keep the revenge cycle going forever in her country and in her heart. It had to stop. By now we had all stopped walking and joined in a little circle around Chantal as we listened to the rest of her story.

Chantal felt God was saying to her in the midst of her murder plan, *Either you forgive and receive forgiveness or you don't. Let me take care of you and your hatred—or give up your freedom, your joy and peace, and live the rest of your life in resentment and bitterness.*

What enabled Chantal to ask the murderer's forgiveness was remembering her shared identity with all human beings. They hate, we hate, and then we all crave revenge. We are all potential murderers.

At that moment, hearing Chantal's quiet but powerful words, I realized I am guilty of the sin of pride and the firm conviction that "I'm not like them." But I *am* like them. I have carried murderous thoughts and cravings on my yoke but hide behind the fact that I've never yielded to them. But that does not make me more righteous than those who have yielded.

We are all sinners in need of forgiveness; the ground at the cross is level.

I will never forget the power of Chantal's humble testimony of forgiveness and its resulting freedom for her soul. With salvation through Jesus, we, the Rwandans, the Israelites, and this reluctant-to-forgive mother can give up our cravings for revenge that enslave us. God's promise is "to let the oppressed go free and to break every yoke." When we step out of that yoke we can then say, "I'm free! Thank God, I'm free at last."

Thirteen

CRAVING FORGIVENESS AND RELIEF FROM GUILT

IF ONE WERE RESEARCHING A PERFECT DIET FOR THE SOUL, the most important nutrients would be confession and forgiveness.

We confess because we feel guilt and shame about a wrong behavior. We feel guilt because of the wrong itself, and we feel shame because we fear we may not be worthy of forgiveness.

Shame makes us hide in the shadows, terrified we'll be found out. The cure for shame is coming out of the shadows and believing we are worthy of forgiveness.

The cure for guilt is not denying the wrong but confessing it as a wrong and then asking to be forgiven. When forgiveness is given, our souls experience the health-producing sense of physical and emotional well-being we all deeply crave.

If the two major health nutrients for our souls are confession and forgiveness, why are so many of us living malnourished soul-lives? The answer is the same one noted twentieth-century British writer and Christian G. K. Chesterton gave when he was asked, "What is wrong with the world?"

Chesterton replied simply, "I am."

That is an interesting confession. Is he saying the world would be a better place if he were a better person? Is he admitting to a certain soul malnourishment that could benefit from a change in diet? It would be presumptuous for me to speculate about Chesterton's interior world, but his confession causes me to speculate about my own; it causes me to realize I, too, am a part of what is wrong with the world.

I was raised to be a confessor. A part of my childhood bedtime routine was to answer my mother's question, "Do you have anything you want to confess?"

I always had something; I had thought bad thoughts, I copied off Sharon's paper on the math test, I cheated just a tiny bit when I reported my spelling score, or I sneaked the liver off my plate and held it under the table for Chelsey (my always-eager-to-help dog). With my mother's guidance, I would confess each wrongdoing and ask Jesus to forgive me. Together we would say 1 John 1:9: "If we confess our sins, He is faithful and just to forgive us our sins and to cleanse us from all unrighteousness" (NKJV).

I loved that routine. By the time my mother switched off the light and I crawled into bed, I felt like a "new woman." I was no longer burdened by guilt or shame; I knew I was forgiven. That is the power of confession. That's the food our soul craves.

The Downside of Keeping Up Appearances

For believers who do not come from a Catholic background or didn't have a mother like mine, the practice of confession may seem foreign. It may also feel intrusive. Many of us feel our interior world is a personal matter that we protect by silence and at times, private guilt. The bottom-line thought for many of us is, *My life and what goes on in it is nobody's business.*

But let's consider the consequences of that choice as we take a peek into a carefully protected private life. He wrote wildly passionate letters to his wife's secretary and later made moves on his own assistant. His wife had her behind-closed-doors passion with several lovers, including another woman. This unorthodox marriage arrangement was simplified by sleeping in separate wings—of the White House. What couple are we talking about? Franklin and Eleanor Roosevelt!

Why have we not heard of most of the Roosevelts' extracurricular activities until recently? In the 1930s the press did not pry into the private lives of politicians. They were judged by what they accomplished for the good of the governed. Everything else was nobody's business.

Now, in this age of media intrusion and easy access to rapid communication through Twitter, blogging, and Facebook (to name a few), everyone knows what once was "nobody's business." Only for a few decades did the secret of FDR's happy marriage remain a secret.

I have no idea how the Roosevelts dealt with their moral failings, but I do know that for anyone, the lack of personal confession and the refusal to be held accountable feeds the drive for continued wrongdoing. In time, the price of not confessing can give way to a sense of entitlement that may envelop the soul with the message, *You deserve more . . . and that* more *is right here in front of you. Take it . . .*

As I write, the misdeeds of the rich and famous are making screaming headlines, including this one from California: GOVERNOR'S SECRET LOVE CHILD REVEALED AFTER TEN YEARS.

Keeping the ink flowing, a housekeeper in a high-end hotel has accused a world leader in international finance of raping her.

An earlier scandal that tapped into the public fury, especially of most women, was the denial, and then the acknowledgment, of a love child fathered by a US senator whose wife was dying of cancer during the affair.

Most of us do not fall into the categories of the rich and famous whose malnourished souls became public; we hope to keep ours private—and often succeed in that secrecy. Many of those who have yet to realize their souls' need of cleansing confession choose instead to busy themselves with keeping up the appearance of acceptability.

I love the BBC classic series *Keeping Up Appearances*. One of the main characters is Hyacinth Bucket (pronounced "Bouquet"), a tireless social climber whose efforts to impress and rise above her "rank" fail continuously and hilariously. In one episode when Hyacinth is planning to repaint her kitchen, she struggles between two colors: Angel Gabriel Blue or Lucifer Gray. She decides to seek the advice of her vicar and asks if he could come to the house. She hesitates because her husband, Richard, has itchy toes, and she does not want the vicar to think her husband has a fungus. She ultimately does invite the vicar but lies to explain Richard's toe troubles, claiming he has gout, a foot disorder known to afflict people in the upper class.

I know few people, including myself, who do not work at keeping up appearances. We don't want anyone to witness the extent to which we can be selfish, controlling, insensitive, and self-centered. We want to appear to be unconditionally gracious, kind, and unprejudiced persons who are capable of forgiving the weaknesses and bad behaviors of others. If we were able to do all that, there is no doubt the world would be a better place. Since I am so often unable to successfully keep up those appearances, and since I frequently fail to be gracious and forgiving, I can only sidle in next to Chesterton and say, "Me too. I'm part of what's wrong with the world."

Craving Normalcy, Balance, and the Removal of Guilt

All this discussion about the degree to which we fall short of being good citizens eager to make the world a better place is discouraging. And not only is it discouraging, but it also makes us feel guilty, thinking we should do better. Most of us really do try, but something human happens and we have to start over.

So we narrow our sense of responsibility and concentrate instead on our own little world of family, friends, and business associates. Sometimes I'm a great mother. At times I was a great wife. Occasionally I'm a great grandmother. But all too often I'm an unavailable friend. The reality is sometimes I do it all well; so do you. But when we don't, what's the answer? Let's consider confession.

Confession is deeply anchored in the very core of our being. All known civilizations have had some kind of confession ritual that led to forgiveness. Why? Because everyone craves the return to balance and normalcy that occurs when one confesses and is then forgiven, and those troubling feelings of guilt are removed.

Our psychological makeup requires us to confess our wrongdoing to others in order to heal our souls and those we've hurt. When I worked as a mental health professional, it was my joy one day to hear a dad say to his eighteen-year-old son, "I've been too hard on you. I expected too much. I've withheld my love and approval of you since you were a child. I am so sorry. Now I want to say what is truly in my heart: I'm proud of you. Will you forgive me for being so demanding and inflexible? I love you, son . . . more than I ever dared to show or say."

But before this dad could make his confession, he had to address the anger he felt toward his own father. That father had never said, "I love you," had never said, "I'm proud of you." He had only said, "You don't do anything right." Without his realizing it, he had repeated that pattern of a dysfunctional father-son relationship with his own son.

The eighteen-year-old's dad first needed to heal his soul of all the unexpressed hurt and anger he felt toward his own father before he could heal the relationship with his son. With the photograph of his no-longer-living dad in front of him, he read to him a letter he had written in which he poured out his feelings about all the years of personal abuse that had caused his soul to wither and feel powerless and unworthy. That acknowledgment of pain, followed by the confession that for years he had wished his dad dead, freed him to then ask forgiveness from his own son.

Our mental health is restored through confession; certainly our spiritual health is dependent upon it. Our need to confess has its root in God's provision for the forgiveness of sin when the first couple disobeyed in the garden of Eden and the stain of their sin covered the earth. God immediately put into place a ritual of confession and forgiveness that would alleviate the consequences of sin of guilt and shame.

Knowing how beneficial confession is for our souls, the natural question to ask is, *Why do we fight against what is so healing?* It would seem we can't admit our own guilt, even to ourselves. We would rather deny it. We would rather expend our energy in keeping up appearances. The price we pay is anguishingly expressed by King David in the thirty-second psalm:

> *When I refused to confess my sin,*
> *my body wasted away,*
> *and I groaned all day long.*
>
> *Day and night your hand of discipline*
> *was heavy on me.*
> *My strength evaporated like water in*
> *the summer heat.*
>
> *Finally, I confessed all my sins to you*
> *and stopped trying to hide my guilt.*
> *I said to myself, "I will confess my*
> *rebellion to the LORD."*
> *And you forgave me! All my guilt*
> *is gone. (vv. 3–5)*

We would assume King David was writing about his sins of murder and adultery and his efforts to keep them from public scrutiny. Keeping up appearances worked for him until, over time, his guilt became overwhelming. He had no more emotional or physical stamina to fight against the conviction of his debilitating sin. He didn't go to his personal shrink for that confession. He fell before the God of all creation and David confessed it all; and God forgave it all.

Praying the Ultimate Prayer of Confession

Though confessing our failings to another human being can be beneficial in that it allows us to make amends and establish new ways of behaving, our forgiveness in that situation is limited. Why? Because only God has the power to forgive sin. Only he has the power to remove the sin stain from our fractured souls and make them clean and whole. Only he could cleanse and forgive King David's sin.

So what is my part in seeking to remove the sin stain from my fractured soul? It is to make the ultimate prayer of confession that could say, "God, thank you for sending Jesus to die for my sin. I confess that I am a sinner. Please forgive me and cleanse me from all the sins of my past and the sins of my present. I believe you and receive you into the deepest regions of my soul. Thank you for loving me. Thank you for forgiving me."

There is no confession more crucially important for our lives than receiving God's forgiveness through faith in Christ. There is, however, another important issue for us to settle. It lies in the answer to the question, *What's wrong with the world?* As someone already freed from the penalty of sin, why did G. K. Chesterton still say he was a part of what's wrong with the world, and why do I share in that "wrong" today?

I share in it because although I am a cleansed and forgiven Christ follower, I'm still not perfect, and the world may suffer the consequences of my imperfect behavior. As long as I'm on this earth, my humanity will be at odds with what I know to be Christlike.

Justification and Sanctification

That being the case, let's take refuge in two liberating doctrines we read throughout Scripture—lessons I was spoon-fed as a child. (I had no idea that diet of God's Word was responsible for enabling me to believe I was not a bad kid and that forgiveness followed confession.) The grown-up words for those doctrines are *justification* and *sanctification*.

Justification means God says I'm no longer a sinner even though I keep on sinning. That is a reality because Jesus took the sin and freed me from its penalty. Simply put, because of Jesus, God no longer sees me as a sinner.

If that's the reality, why do I confess my sins? I ask forgiveness because I want to take ownership of my wrongdoing. I need to admit it. I need to say I'm sorry. I'm not wired to pretend I didn't cheat on a math test. I am wired to confess it and to experience the healing of forgiveness.

Sanctification is the process God uses in "growing me up" and leading me to an ever-increasing level of maturity. This goes on for the rest of my life. I experienced the process of sanctification with the realization that cheating on a math test was wrong and not worth the feelings of guilt and shame. I will never lose the temptation to cheat, but maturity will enable me to make a more Christlike choice. Maturity will also encourage me to feel an ever-increasing dependence on the power of the Holy Spirit who lives within me.

What happens when I am immature and do not seek the empowerment of the Holy Spirit when I face temptation? What happens when I yield to un-Christlike behavior and enter into the very sin for which I have asked forgiveness many times before? I take responsibility for that behavior, confess that I was not Christlike, and thank God yet again that I am his cleansed and forgiven child.

We desperately need the diet of confession and forgiveness. There is no more nutritious soul food on earth than what God provides daily for his creation. May I suggest you memorize Psalm 65:3 as a megavitamin to be included in your daily soul food regime? You can expect powerfully restorative results. How do I know? I learned it as a child: "Though we are overwhelmed by our sins, you forgive them all."

Fourteen

FEELING HOMESICK

MY DAUGHTER BETH'S WEDDING IN MARION, OHIO, ON JUNE 15, 2011, turned out to be a flawlessly flowing ceremony where everything reflected good planning as well as God's tangible touch of love and grace. The days leading up to the event had been poignantly sweet and full of fun and laughter, and the day of the wedding itself was perfect. I love my new son-in-law Dave Claborn, and (obviously) so does Beth. As she hugged me before leaving for her honeymoon, she said, "This whole day has been an over-the-top *more!*"

As mother of the bride and matron of honor, I wholeheartedly agreed. And the good times didn't stop there. My happy duty after the ceremony was to instruct my two grandsons—Alec, fourteen, and Ian, sixteen—how to take care of me for the next three days. They both did a masterful job of tending to my every need, but I simply must share a supersize *more* experience that Alec's caretaking provided.

I don't remember a time in my life when I have not had a deep craving for one of those big, sweeping front porches enveloped by huge shade trees. Marion has a gazillion porches that fit that description and filled my heart with longing. One evening I asked Alec if he would take me for a walk. Ever the accommodating young man, he readily agreed, and we set out. Within moments we came upon a house with a to-die-for porch.

Alec is exceedingly literal, and for years he has been mystified by my occasional off-the-wall behavior. When I suggested we go sit on that porch for just a few minutes, he patiently explained that we could not do that because "we don't know those people; you can't just go sit on a stranger's porch."

We walked on.

But then a second to-die-for porch appeared; I headed for it only to be gently led back to the sidewalk by my long-suffering grandson. I began whining a bit and pointed out that the gorgeous elm trees with their leaves shushing the breeze were too good to pass up. Suddenly Alec's face broke into a huge grin. "I know a perfect porch with chairs, and no one lives there."

Only one block farther I found myself on one of the most spacious and gorgeous porches I ever saw. Enveloped by huge trees on perfectly manicured grounds, the two of us sat blissfully chatting for more than an hour. It was one of those supersize *more* experiences I will forever hold dear, right alongside the memories of Beth's wedding day.

In case you are ever in Marion, and you, too, need the

solace of a perfect porch, make your way to the home of our twenty-ninth president, Warren G. Harding, who, I have since learned, made many political speeches from that very porch. I love it that his hometown is preserving the house and the grounds, thus providing porch time for a grateful grandma, a relieved grandson, and anyone else who needs to just drop by and "sit a spell."

A Longing for Satisfaction

If I were to get to the root of my porch craving, I think it would be obvious that a porch says "home" to me. As a preacher's daughter who lived in a number of parsonages, some fine and some not so fine, the common feature of them all was a porch. Those porches provided solace for my soul as I engaged in deep thought, meaningful conversation, and, when I was old enough, a kiss or two.

My grandparents' home in Cortez, Colorado, was on East Montezuma Avenue. That house, built in 1910, has a memory-filled and amazing porch where my grandparents sat as newlyweds, new parents, active professionals, and finally as frail persons whose life experiences were narrowed to remembrances of things past. Their porch was a place where I, too, created both childhood and adult-years memories, including the sad memory from ten years ago when I had to sell the house. Before I left my grandparents' porch for the last time, I sat in my grandfather's old wooden rocker, drank a cup of tea, and quietly commemorated the decades of family exchanges, quiet reveries, and finally the loss of the two generations that preceded mine. All those loved ones are gone now, but the porch remains, and will continued to do so, even if only in my mind's storehouse of treasured memories.

That's why my craving for a porch is fed by more than a structural porch itself. At times I am simply longing for the familiar, the comforting, the security-producing feel of what was. Sitting on a porch becomes my trusted link to my deepest craving that is home—past, present, and future.

Of course, a porch is not a required link to connect my heart to home. The home craving does not need a link; it simply exists, lying quietly on the floor of the soul . . . waiting.

Waiting for what? Satisfaction.

My dear friend Mary Graham was born in Oklahoma in a little town named Picher. At its peak in 1926, Picher sat at the center of the tristate mining district and was the lead and zinc capital of the world. For decades it thrived as a place where families lived and created memories. Then, in 1983, it was declared one of the most toxic places in America, initially because of the mine waste that was contaminating the water. Studies later showed that about a third of children in the area had elevated lead levels in their blood.

Recently, a state study showed numerous sites in the area where the ground was at risk of collapse because of the vast underground network of caves left by the mining. There had been multiple cave-ins over the years causing property damage and at least one death as a motorist drove into a gaping hole.

Officials announced a federally funded voluntary buy-out to all residents who wished to leave Picher. Everyone left, except for six households that stayed. They watch now as track hoes and dump trucks systematically destroy the town's buildings and haul them away to who knows where.

Mary told me recently her brother John wants to buy Picher. She asked him why on earth he'd want to buy a contaminated town with nothing left but a few buildings and a lot of sinkholes. His response was, "Mickey Mantle lived here. His dad and our dad worked in the mines together. Our high school team won a state football championship here. We all went to Sunday school at Union Church. Mary, this is our *home*."

To Mary's brother, buying Picher might satisfy his home craving, a feeling he might not even be able to name. If he owned Picher, then home could not be plowed under by a bulldozer. As far as he is able, he wants to protect the place they know as home, preserving its memories as well as his own.

House versus Home

What are the feelings of home? Many of us make a distinction between house and home. Real estate ads offer houses for sale, not homes. In his book *Staying Put: Making a Home in a Restless World*, writer Scott Russell Sanders says a "house is a garment easily put off or on, casually bought and sold; a home is skin. Merely change houses and you will be disoriented; change homes and you bleed." Frederick Buechner echoed the same theme in *Godric*: "When a man leaves home, he leaves behind some scrap of his heart."

Among the sweetest and most warmly nostalgic elements of home are the traditions we hold dear. For example, in Pat Wenger's home one of the Christmas traditions that excited her little boys the entire month of December were the Christmas stockings. Beginning on December 1 she hung four stockings on the mantel. (The fourth stocking was for Czar, their dog who loved his very own stocking as much as the boys loved theirs.) Each morning throughout the month of December, the boys and Czar would race to their stockings to discover their new present for the day. The kids would find anything from baseball cards to a flashlight or a pack of gum. Czar would find a bone that he immediately hid behind various pieces of furniture throughout the house. Pat discovered hidden bones well into the month of July. This Christmas tradition is being honored and preserved now by Pat's married sons as they hang Christmas stockings for their own kids.

One of my treasured Christmas memories as I grew up in the Pacific Northwest was the tradition my father and I had of heading into the woods to carefully select and then chop down our Christmas tree. That tree came either from our own rural property or from the woods of various church members. After chopping, we began the ceremonial "dragging." I always wanted to be the one to drag the tree from the woods to our car. Dad patiently allowed me to stumble through this physical exertion until finally, panting in triumph, I allowed Dad to secure the tree on top of the car.

Once home I nearly fell under the weight of heavenly smells coming from the kitchen. Mom had cooked while we labored and, oh my, what a feast she presented: all my favorite foods. But the greatest and the best were her chocolate brownies. To this day, the smell of brownies takes me back to the memory of the home where I reveled in a good day's "tree chop" and my very own "tree drag."

When I married Ken Meberg and we moved to California, we got our first Christmas tree from the lot of a neighborhood supermarket. It was an unsettling experience for me. I made no effort to drag the tree the few feet required to secure it to the top of our car. And I knew not to expect the smell of brownies when I opened our apartment door.

It is not only the memory of sweet traditions we associate with home but the various smells as well. Certainly the smell of chocolate brownies is a favorite of mine, but so, too, is the smell of freshly cut hay, especially alfalfa. Being raised in the midst of many farms, my favorite time of summer was mowing season; I believe the richly pungent smell of alfalfa should be packaged into a perfume. During those summers I would go out to Harry Hooper's farm with my father so he could help Harry "put up" the hay. While they worked I lay in the alfalfa field breathing myself into a happily aromatic faint.

The closest I can come now to feeling that nostalgic pleasure is when my yard is mowed. It's nice but doesn't hold a candle to the smell of alfalfa. (I honestly wish my yard was alfalfa, but apparently there's this chokehold rule from the homeowners' association . . .)

Pangs of Homesickness

Home will always be with us wherever we go simply because it lives inside us, offering up feelings. Of course, those feelings may not always be sweetly nostalgic. We may associate pain, hurt, and sadness with home. When my father left home at the age of fourteen to work in a sawmill, he sent a portion of his paycheck to his mother to help with the rearing of his nine brothers and sisters. Dad never went back home; he never wanted to. Home to him represented everything he wanted to leave behind—and he did just that.

For many, the memory of home may not necessarily be sad but is remembered as a place of uncertainty, mystery, and longing. In her short story "The Fullness of Life," American author Edith Wharton wrote that a person's life is like "a great house full of rooms, most of which remain unseen: and in the innermost room, the holy of holies, the soul sits alone and waits for a footstep that never comes."

Great literature lends itself to personal application as well as to endless speculation about the meanings attached to its various themes. In Wharton's story we absorb the haunting images of the soul who sits alone waiting for the footstep that never comes and ask, *Why are you waiting for what does not enter the room?*

Like those characters who waited endlessly and futilely for Godot, there is a sense of hopelessness in the waiting Wharton describes and yet, maybe not. Perhaps the waiting is a picture of patience; perhaps the character knows that ultimately the footstep *will* come, the wait *will* be rewarded. But during that waiting while knowing, feelings of disillusionment or abandonment may undermine patience and cause the waiting to be even more challenging; ultimately, though, the footstep is heard and the expected one enters the room. Hope was not in vain.

The same theme of waiting is found in this line from

Hermann Hesse's short story *Klingsor's Last Summer*: "Tell me oh you who sit over your full cup, for whom are you still waiting?"

We readers may ask the same question and with a hint of impatience say, "The cup is full; there's no good reason to wait. Get on with it!"

The intense craving for home and the search to satisfy it—listening for the footstep, waiting with a full cup, and creating diversions while we wait—are characteristics we all share. In fact, the characteristics are so common there is a name for our behavior when these feelings surface: we're homesick. Many of us do not know, however, that our home-sickness has little to do with this earth and everything to do with eternity. We just know we want more, crave more, and even a porch can't fully satisfy the craving. Why? Because sooner or later I need to leave the porch to satisfy some other need: food, warmth, a bathroom, sleep.

Again my mother's words come back to me; all the solutions that satisfy every one of my cravings have a beginning, a middle, and an end. The solution works great at first, and then . . .

Why do we have cravings? We're homesick.

Homesick for what? Heaven.

Homesick for whom? God. It is he and he alone who will totally eliminate all our cravings—but not until we're home with him in heaven. As long as we're here on earth, we can only experience partial craving solutions. Our deepest soul knows that because God "has planted eternity in the human heart" (Ecclesiastes 3:11).

And why did God plant eternity in our hearts? "He puts a little of heaven in our hearts so that we'll never settle for less" (2 Corinthians 5:5 MSG). We were created to want more and to never "settle for less." In heaven, all that *more* we've craved on earth will ultimately be returned to us and we will experience total satisfaction. In the meantime, we wait.

Our wait, however, is filled with hopeful anticipation. To begin with, our imaginations are stimulated with expectations of grandeur based upon the words of Jesus, who told his disciples, "In My Father's house are many mansions; if it were not so, I would have told you. I go to prepare a place for you . . . that where I am, there you may be also" (John 14:2–3 NKJV).

Of course, my earthbound mind cannot imagine a mansion without a porch. I can take that image even further and envision Jesus having tea with me on that porch. We'll discuss more of these delicious possibilities in the next chapter on heaven.

Homelessness of the Soul

While we wait on this earth, the most troubling ailment of the soul is not homesickness, because as Christ followers we know the heavenly solution as well as the explanation. The most troubling ailment here is homelessness of the soul. To feel homeless is to have no center, to be unsure if we have an anchor or where we can find it. Feelings of homelessness produce in us a sense of restlessness that senses there is no recognizable place to experience the familiar, the known, the safe. There's not a porch in sight.

Dare I suggest that even Christ followers can lose sight of their assurance of home and join the wandering masses of those suffering homelessness of the soul? Sure, we know better, but . . .

The reality for us all is that we are indeed "strangers and pilgrims on the earth . . . [who] seek a homeland" (Hebrews 11:13–14 NKJV), and sometimes we lose our way. When that happens, we refocus the lens through which we view life, remember we belong to the God of all creation whose love is greater than our prone-to-wander tendencies. And then will come a day when the joyful sounds of our astonished delight will reverberate throughout the universes; the wait is over. We're *home*!

Fifteen

CRAVING HEAVEN

WHAT CAN WE KNOW FOR SURE ABOUT OUR FUTURE HOME IN heaven? What can we expect to experience in the place we have inexplicably craved since the day we were born?

One answer is found in the words Matthew said all Christ followers will hear when we arrive at heaven's gate: "Enter into the joy of your Lord."

What will we find in heaven? Joy!

Fantastic! We all love to be joyful, to be around joyful people, and to feel only joyful emotions. In fact, joy is my favorite emotion. And who is the originator, the source of that joy? God. He is not only joyful himself, but he created in each of us the ability to experience joy as well—joy that runs so deeply throughout our being we can be totally saturated and soaked with its delicious presence. Who will be our continual conduit of joy in heaven? God.

Quite simply and profoundly, heaven is all about joy.

What does it mean that we anticipate living in a totally joyful environment? It means nothing can take our joy away. There will be no depression, disappointment, dissatisfaction, fears, jealousy, insecurity, anger, money problems, or betrayal. And that, of course, is the short list; you can undoubtedly add other emotions that have stolen your joy throughout your earthly life. Can you even imagine an environment so joyful that not a single negative thought or emotion will ever, ever plague you again?

Not only does joy make it impossible to feel sad, it also will be impossible to experience physical pain. Think of it. Not one of us is free of at least some physical discomfort. I have back pain, colitis, and high blood pressure (telltale symptoms of emotional distress, but I'm not sure why). I have friends with pain so debilitating and paralysis so physically limiting they don't have one moment free from its effects. Can you even imagine the joy of being pain-free forever and ever?

Joy not only eliminates the existence of earth's emotional and physical distresses, it also ushers in laughter and lightheartedness. I plan to laugh loud and hard in heaven. Why? God does. How can I make such an assumption? Genesis tells us we are created in the image of God; if the divinely inspired humor-packet were not within us, we'd never be inclined to create humor or respond to it. It would not occur to us. Instead, our Creator passed on to us the inherent ability to appreciate, enjoy, and enter into what produces a laughter response.

I frequently entertain the notion that perhaps a part of our heavenly joy will have also been an earthly joy. I wonder if there might be "carryovers" from here to there simply because some things are too good to leave behind. For example, and I know this sounds trivial, I cannot imagine a perfect and joyful place without watermelon. I love it that God created watermelon. One of my favorite earth memories features watermelon, my dad, and laughter. I'd like to suggest it was a slice of heaven on earth. I've got to share it with you.

As a child my father and I would have watermelon-seed spitting contests. We'd sit outside in the backyard and from our respective lawn chairs attempt to spit the seeds beyond the rope boundary he had set up on the grass. Apparently we were fairly evenly matched because I remember Dad telling me I was on my way to being the best spitter in the state but that he would not easily give up his title. I was coached to push more air behind the seed that just might cause it to fly farther.

One warm summer day in Chino, California, when Dad and I were working on our spitting skills, I was in the lead. In an effort to regain the lead, Dad put extra air velocity behind his seed-spit. In so doing, not only did the seed sail over the rope boundary, so did his top teeth! I'd long been fascinated with Dad's false teeth (uppers and lowers), but never had I seen them put to such delightful comedic use. The uppers sat in the grass alongside the champion seed. Hands down, Dad won. I laughed for hours.

And speaking of food, can we say for sure there will be

great eating in heaven? Is that merely speculation or wishful thinking? Consider these statistics: words about eating, meals, and various foods appear more than a thousand times in the Bible, with the English translation "feast" occurring 187 times.

Let's take a look at a few of these scriptures.

- Shortly before his crucifixion, Jesus said to his disciples, "You have stayed with me in my time of trial. And just as my Father has granted me a Kingdom, I now grant you the right to eat and drink at my table in my Kingdom" (Luke 22:28–30).

- Revelation 19:9 speaks of the "wedding feast of the Lamb." Who will be the bride? We who have placed our faith in the saving act of Jesus on the cross. And where will this supper be held? In heaven.

- Isaiah 25:6 states, "The LORD of Heaven's Armies will spread a wonderful feast for all the people of the world. It will be a delicious banquet with clear, well-aged wine and choice meat."

- At the last supper prior to the crucifixion of Jesus he "took a cup of wine and gave thanks to God for it. Then he said, 'Take this and share it among yourselves. For I will not drink wine

again until the Kingdom of God has come'"
(Luke 22:17–18).

One of my favorite earthly experiences is to share a
meal with people I love. Almost every Sunday after church,
Mary Graham, Ney Bailey, Pat Wenger, Luci Swindoll,
and I go to a "special spot" for brunch. Chuck and Cynthia
Swindoll often join us. We talk, laugh, and stay longer than
anyone else there. Why? We're having fun and enjoying one
another; we are utilizing our God-given capacity to experience pleasure and joy. It is heavenly.

I wonder if, in addition to food, another possible carryover from earth to heaven is animals. I've always found
it appealing that God places a high value on animals.
According to the Genesis account, God decided it was not
good for Adam to be alone so God created animals and
birds for him. Only afterward did God create woman. God
instructed both Adam and Eve to give a name to each of the
many animals in the garden. God didn't tell them to name
the plants, only the animals.

Later on in the book of Genesis, where we read of Noah
and the flood, God told Noah to bring into the ark two of
all living creatures, male and female. God's intention? After
the destruction of all life resulting from the flood, there
would then be new life on a restored earth that included
animals as well as people.

There are scenic beauty spots on this earth that so overwhelm my senses I can hardly breathe, places I think must be leftover Eden beauty. That beauty is no longer perfect, but these places seem so close to perfection it is not hard to imagine the garden the first couple knew.

Not many miles down from Telluride, Colorado, is a fantastic fishing place called Trout Lake. It is one of the deepest lakes in the state and without a doubt one of the coldest. I soon learned not to cast out my fishing line while standing ankle deep in that frigid, snow-fed water. The lake is encircled by the massive Rocky Mountains with an abundance of poplar, spruce, and fir trees. Breathtaking.

In my mind's memory, I still see my mom under one of those trees reading while Dad and I caught rainbow trout so eager to grab our bait we could barely keep up with them. That night, encased in a crispy coat of yellow cornmeal and fried in butter, we ate the fruits (fish) of our labors. Heavenly.

Ken and I honeymooned in Victoria, Canada, with side trips through Banff National Park, where we hiked, picnicked, and often sat in stunned silence at the grandeur of the Canadian Rockies. We both grew up in the Pacific Northwest, and we never took that area's magnificent scenery for granted, but it was nevertheless an easy expectation we counted on. When we moved to Southern California, that daily feeding of scenic beauty was no longer available to us, and the loss created an ache in our souls that I still feel occasionally.

So I say again, all this earthly beauty and grandeur can't be left behind; surely there will be a carryover.

On the other hand, many highly respected theologians believe not in a carryover but a makeover for this earth. They believe that the words of Isaiah 65:17—"Behold, I create new heavens and a new earth" (NKJV)—refer to our present earth that God will make new.

Dr. Randy Alcorn, after twenty-five years of extensive research on what Scripture says about heaven, makes this provocative statement about Eden: "God is not done with Eden. He preserved it not as a museum piece, but as a place that humanity will one day occupy again."[1]

He claims we are homesick for Eden and the redeemed, transfigured, recreated earth-heaven is our ultimate destination.

If these are new thoughts to you, as they were to me, Dr. Alcorn provides these clarifying insights about his view of God's intent for the future of our earth:

Adam was formed from the dust of the earth, forever establishing our connection to the earth (Genesis 2:7). Just as we are made from the earth, so too we are made for the earth. "But," you may object, "Jesus said he was going to prepare a place for us and would take us there to live with him forever" (John 14:2–3). Yes. But what is that place? Revelation 21 makes it clear—it's the New Earth.[2]

What is especially encouraging to me about Dr. Alcorn's research is, not only can we find some carryovers on the restored earth, but also that God has never given up on his original creation. His grace assures me that he never gives up on me but sees me in light of what he intended me to be. He sees the earth the same way—that which he always intended it to be.

In his Book *Creation Regained*, religion professor Albert Wolters wrote,

> God hangs on to his fallen original creation and salvages it. He refuses to abandon the work of his hands—in fact, he sacrifices his own Son to save his original project. Humankind, who has botched its original mandate and the whole creation along with it, is given another chance in Christ, we are reinstated as God's managers on earth. The original good creation is to be restored.[3]

What does Wolters mean when he says we will be "reinstated as God's managers on earth"? What are we going to manage? For those many believers who have quietly confessed their fear that heaven may be boring, the answer to that question is reassuring as well as intriguing. Relying again on Dr. Alcorn's research, he builds a biblical argument that we are all going to be very busy in heaven, happily and fulfillingly busy. Here are some of his scripturally supported points of view.

- We are told in Hebrews 11:10 and 13:14 that heaven is a city. What is a city? A place where there are buildings. What goes on in those buildings? People going about their God-given tasks and making decisions for the glory of the city. Those decisions may have to do with art, music, athletics, and various other pleasure-producing events.
- Hebrews 11:16 describes heaven as a country. Countries have territories, rulers, and citizens who no longer defend their territory but share it with all who visit their country.[4]

When God promises a new earth, the word *earth* must mean we can expect earthly things to be present. Things like mountains, trees, flowers, streams, and lakes filled with unpolluted water. Again, that list could go on and on. Dare I suggest that the new earth may have watermelon?

Some might say these earthly carryovers can't be part of our heavenly home. I ask, why not?

First Corinthians 15:40–44 tells us we will have resurrection bodies; each of us will have a new, perfectly functioning body that is free from pain or disease. Surely that means we can eat heavenly food!

After his resurrection Jesus had a new body. He appeared and disappeared, and he joined the disciples in eating. He was no longer encased in a body with limitations; after he arose from the dead he had totally divine potentialities. So, too, will we have a new resurrected body. I say "fantastic!"

With this expanded view of heaven and all its divine potentialities for activity, we can discard the fear of spending eternity plucking a harp on some celestial cloud. Instead we will be delightedly busy and fully satisfied in all our God-created purposes. Boredom is earthly thinking, a mind-set that will have no carryover to heaven.

I often scold myself about those times I argue against what can only be explained as the mystery of God. There are numerous scriptures that remind me his ways are "past finding out" and totally beyond my comprehension. I am instructed to see God's ways through the eyes of faith and not the narrow version of what translates as "reasonable" to me. Even Ben Franklin said, "The way to see by faith is to shut the eye of reason."

A book that, as of this writing, remains on the *New York Times* best-seller list is an account that may cause some of the reading public to shut the eye of reason. Nevertheless, the book speaks to the eagerness people have to believe even in that which is a stretch for the "reasonable mind." It has to do with heaven and a little boy's report of being there. The book is entitled *Heaven Is for Real*.

In 2003 little Colton Burpo, not yet four years old, survived an emergency appendectomy. Afterward he told his parents he had left his body during the surgery, and he authenticated that claim by describing what his parents were doing in another part of the hospital while he was being operated on.

He talked of visiting heaven, and he relayed stories told to him by people he saw there whom he had not met in his life on earth. He tells of meeting long-departed family members, including the especially astonishing experience of meeting a sister who was lost through a miscarriage. No one had told Colton of that baby lost to a miscarriage. Hearing him say he had met that child in heaven who recognized Colton as her brother was astounding to Colton's parents.

He also described the vibrancy of the multitudes of colors in heaven, of Jesus, the angels, how "really, really big" God is, and "how much they love us."

Several weeks before my husband Ken died, he had a vivid dream. He said he dreamed he was standing next to a beautiful lake with a gently rippling current. Across the lake were a number of people waving to him and encouraging him to come "over." At first he was not sure who was waving him on. Gradually, though, he began to recognize them.

One was his father, who had died when Ken was twelve. Standing next to his dad was my mother. Standing next to her was a little girl. Initially, Ken didn't know who she was but gradually realized she was Joani, our baby who had died when she was fifteen days old.

I've never written about this or even shared it with anyone; but little Colton's heaven experience expands my sense of possibilities and wonder about all that seems far too mysterious for my adult mind. How could Ken see a little girl who went to heaven as an infant? How could he know she is Joani? Perhaps I once again need reminding that God's ways are higher than mine. And not only are they higher than mine, but I also have a mental ceiling that limits my ability to rise above my understanding of all the mystery that is God.

The question I need to ask is not how Ken knew, how Colton knew, and how others who have also been granted glimpses of heaven knew. Instead I need to ask, *Why is it so hard to believe that "heaven is for real"?* There is a gravitational pull that keeps many of us tethered to this earth's belief that whatever is miraculous or supernatural may be suspect. We think it can't be true; there must be some trickery or false representation involved. Either that, or we assume people are simply naïve, ill-informed, and, like children, believe in fairy tales.

C. S. Lewis wrote, "We want something else which can hardly be put into words; to be united with the beauty we see, to pass into it, to receive it into ourselves, to bathe in it, to become part of it."

That "something else" is the place for which we were sovereignly designed to live forever and ever in the presence of God our Creator and Jesus our Savior. That place is heaven and . . . heaven is for real.

Sixteen

ONE MORE WORD

WHEN MARK TWAIN'S CHARACTER HUCK FINN STRUGGLED WITH HIS sense of wanting to do the right thing in life but not always succeeding, he finally put that struggle to rest with these thoughts:

> I knowed very well I had done wrong, and I see it warn't no use for me to try to learn to do right; a body that can't get started right when he's little, ain't got no show— when the pinch comes there ain't nothing to back him up and keep him to his work, and so he gets beat . . . then says I, what's the use you learning to do right, when it's troublesome to do right and ain't no trouble to do wrong, and the wages is just the same? I was stuck. I couldn't answer that. So I reckoned I wouldn't bother no more about it, but after this always do whichever come handiest at the time.[1]

Undoubtedly, many of us agree the easiest way to deal with human inclinations that are wrong is to simply give in because it's easier to "do whichever come handiest at the time." With his typical insight and verbal eloquence, Huck stated the moral dilemma of the human race. *What does one do about the internal struggle with good versus bad?* Huck's advice to himself was to give in and not fight it. He justified that decision by noting that his childhood had given him no teaching on moral issues, so what could be expected from such an impoverished background?

Most of us "know better" and feel guilty about our wrong choices. Each time we blow it we feel defeated, asking ourselves why it is so much easier to give in than to fight for right.

The apostle Paul expressed his own interior battle in Romans 7 saying: "I don't really understand myself, for I want to do what is right, but I don't do it. Instead, I do what I hate. But if I know that what I am doing is wrong. . . ."

We suffer from the sin tattoo that was imprinted upon our human souls the moment Adam and Eve gave in because that decision "came handiest at the time." Besides that, it was appealing and seemed worth the risk.

As long as we are earth-tethered to this place yet to be "home," we will experience internal conflict over right and wrong with the temptation to take the path of least resistance. At first it may seem worth the risk.

In this book I have not written about the most commonly discussed and socially apparent craving issues like alcohol, drugs, pornography, or gambling. I hardly need to tell you the anguish of those addictions for your life and the lives of those who love you. There was a beginning point when you decided the substance or the behavior was worth the risk. Perhaps with all your soul you now regret having taken that risk.

For any of you whose cravings seem stronger than your resistance, I want to remind you of what your heavenly Father is feeling toward you at this very moment, and what he encourages you to do. We learn about the Father's feelings from a famous story Jesus told in Luke 15.

A young man had gone from riches to rags in a short period of time. While his inheritance money lasted, the young man lived the high life of wine, women, and song. When the money was gone, so, too, were the parties. With nothing to eat, no clothes to wear, and no home in which to live, the young man chose to come home in disgrace and poverty, planning to beg his father for forgiveness and hope to live in his house as a servant. So, dreading the rejection, judgment, and anger he felt he deserved but feeling he had no other choice, he returned home.

Luke 15:20 describes the father's response the moment he sees his son in the distance, making his way home.

And while he was still a long way off, his father saw him coming. Filled with love and compassion, he ran to his son, embraced him, and kissed him.

221

This picture of a father overjoyed at the sight of his wayward boy, who not only received forgiveness but was given a huge welcome-home party of celebration, is the picture of our Father, our homecoming. Jesus told that story so we might know our Father receives our confession, forgives our sin, and continues to love us beyond all expectation. In addition to that, he throws a party and invites all the family and neighbors to celebrate our arrival.

Isaiah 62:5 says, "God will rejoice over you as a bridegroom rejoices over his bride."

My prayer for you is that you not miss the party. It's at "home" . . . in your honor.

NOTES

Chapter 2: Craving More Romance

1. Gustave Flaubert, *Madame Bovary* (New York: Barnes and Noble Books, 1993), 62.

Chapter 3: Why Do I Crave *You*?

1. Andrew M. Colman, *A Dictionary of Psychology* (Norwalk, CT: Oxford University Press, 2006), 431.

Chapter 7: Needing More from Friendship

1. The following account is drawn from Isabella Hatkoff, Craig Hatkoff, Paula Kahumbu and Peter Greste, *Owen and Mzee: The True Story of a Remarkable Friendship* (New York: Scholastic Press, 2006).

Chapter 9: Yearning for More Meaning in Life

1. Leo Tolstoy, *Confession* (New York: W. W. Norton Co., 1996), 42.

Chapter 15: Craving Heaven
1. Randy Alcorn, *Heaven* (Wheaton, Ill: Tyndale, 2004), 78.
2. Ibid.
3. Albert M. Wolters, *Creation Regained: Biblical Basics for a Reformational Worldview* (Grand Rapids: Eermans, 1985), 58.
4. Ibid., xx.

Chapter 16: One More Word
1. Mark Twain, *Adventures of Huckleberry Finn* (1885; repr., Boston: Houghton Mifflin, 1958), 78.

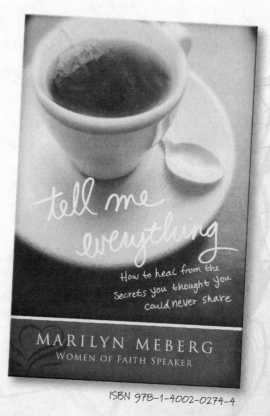